Western
Fly-Fishing
Strategies

BOOKS BY
CRAIG MATHEWS

Fly Patterns of Yellowstone
(with John Juracek)

Fishing Yellowstone Hatches
(with John Juracek)

The Yellowstone Fly-Fishing Guide
(with Clayton Molinero)

Western Fly-Fishing Strategies

Western
Fly-Fishing
Strategies

CRAIG MATHEWS
Illustrations by Rod Walinchus

The Lyons Press
Guilford, Connecticut
An Imprint of The Globe Pequot Press

The Lyons Press is an imprint of The Globe Pequot Press.

10 9 8 7 6 5 4 3 2 1

Printed in the United States of America

Designed by Desktop Miracles, Inc. Dallas, Texas

ISBN-13: 978-1-59228-846-5
ISBN-10: 1-59228-846-4

**The Library of Congress has previously cataloged
an earlier (hardcover) edition as follows:**

Mathews, Craig
Western fly-fishing strategies / Craig Mathews.
    p.   cm.
Includes bibliographical references and index.
ISBN 1-55821-641-3
    1. Trout fishing—West (U.S.)   2. Fly fishing—West (U.S.)   I. Title.
SH688.U6M385 1998
799.1'757'0978—dc21

                                                            97–23800
                                                            CIP

DEDICATION

For my wife, Jackie,
and my parents, Bob and Lillian Mathews,
who've always encouraged and supported my fly-fishing habit.

C O N T E N T S

ACKNOWLEDGMENTS

I'd like to thank many friends who've shared their fly-fishing techniques and strategies with me.

Special thanks to Larry Dech for introducing me long ago to western fly fishing. Thanks to Dan Daufel, Doug Daufel, Larry Dech, John Juracek, Harry Mayo, Clayton Molinero, Rowan Nyman, Phil Takatsuno, and Ken Takata for the photographs.

Thanks to Jim Babb and Verlyn Klinkenborg for their ideas and assistance organizing this.

Finally, thanks to Anja Schmidt and Nick Lyons, who encouraged me, were always there with help and ideas, and made this book possible.

The Magic of Western Waters

W estern fly fishing helps preserve our capacity for wonder. It teaches us to see, smell, and feel the miracles of stream life, with beauty and serenity all around us as we pursue wild trout.

Much has been written of the rivers, lakes, and streams I call my home waters. From my fly-tying room window looking out toward the west and Lionhead Mountain, I can see smoke curling out of Charlie Brooks's chimney. Charlie and I spent many days during his recuperation from a heart attack discussing his books *The Living River* and *Fishing Yellowstone Waters*. These, and his others—*Larger Trout for the Western Fly Fisherman*, *Nymph Fishing for Larger Trout*, and *The Trout and the Stream*—are about his love affairs with the rivers, lakes, and streams here in Yellowstone country. Charlie passed away several years ago, but his books help preserve the magic of western fly fishing. Other authors, such as Howard Back, Ray Bergman, Joe Brooks, Nick Lyons, and Ernest Schwiebert, have also given readers insight into the unique, exciting, and magical experience that the trout waters of the place I call home offer anglers.

My home waters are those in Yellowstone Park, southwestern Montana, and eastern Idaho, an area once referred to as The Golden Triangle. This includes the Madison, Henry's Fork, Gallatin, and Yellowstone Rivers. I've been fishing these waters for nearly three decades and have guided on them for almost 20 years.

As an outfitter and owner of a fly shop in West Yellowstone, Montana, I'm familiar with the difficulties visiting anglers face when fishing western waters, because I've faced those same difficulties myself. To help these anglers I've written books about fly patterns and hatches, and a guidebook to the waters of Yellowstone Park. Because western fly fishing is a game of strategies, it is the intention of this book to help you understand them.

Fly fishermen new to this area's rivers, lakes, sloughs, and ponds are often overwhelmed by the breadth of opportunities to catch big, wild trout on public waters. Most are amazed at the size, speed, and force of our larger rivers, and that big trout often rise to small insects on these flows.

The area within a 100-mile radius of where I live contains nearly 2,000 miles of trout streams and hundreds of lakes, sloughs, and ponds, 90 percent of which are open to the public. There is no place in the world with as much accessible trout water in such a small space. Fly fishers can expect to do well here and throughout the West—provided they know and use the proper strategies and techniques at the right time. Pure luck and successful angling seldom go hand in hand.

One spring more than 25 short fly-fishing seasons ago my fishing companion, outdoor photographer Larry Dech, promised me big, fall-run, wild brown trout on the longest undammed river in North America—the Yellowstone. I read about western fly fishing and tied flies all summer. When October arrived we strolled into Martin's Railroad Diner in Livingston and I pronounced myself "ready" for western angling. After two days on the Yellowstone River near Emigrant and one morning on the Gallatin River just south of Gallatin Gateway, I realized I was unprepared for the angling situations I was facing on that first trip.

Thereafter, Larry and I took yearly trips to Yellowstone country. After several years I finally convinced my wife, Jackie, to come along. Little did I know that by the end of her first Montana trip we'd be scheming to move West. We had to learn, master, and fish all of Yellowstone's and Montana's waters. Within a month we'd purchased a house, sight unseen, in West Yellowstone, and taken jobs there: she as a police dispatcher and I as the police chief of this small town.

We set out to fish it all. Charlie Brooks warned us that it could not be done in two lifetimes: There was just too much water. We were determined to prove him wrong, but we've not yet scratched the surface.

Western waters are unique. We have large and brawling rivers such as the Madison; tiny, intimate spring creeks that feed larger streams along their courses; big lakes such as Yellowstone, full of native cutthroat trout; and small emerald beaver ponds teeming with huge brook trout, thought only available in Labrador.

In the past 25 years western fly fishing has matured and changed dramatically. Gone are the days when almost any fly would produce. A covey of quail never hunted holds for a good pointing dog once, but rarely twice. After this the birds become "wild," flushing out of range. The same with trout here. With increased angling pressure, year-round and catch-and-release fishing from increasingly sophisticated anglers, our quarry has become less easily gulled by trout flies. No longer is pure luck enough, as it was in the "good ol' days" when anglers took home plenty of wild western trout—and then began to wonder where all the fish had gone. Today's progressive fish management has resulted in more wild trout per mile than we have seen in decades. But given the maturation of western fly fishing, opportunity needs to be accompanied by preparation to achieve anything like the catches of the past.

To know western trout water is to be successful on that water. Nowhere else must anglers use so many strategies on such a wide variety of water during so many weather conditions to be successful. That's where I hope this book will come in handy for trout fishermen on our western waters.

PART ONE

The
Western Way

CHAPTER 1

The Plan

C harlie Brooks, Yellowstone fishing legend and author, once said, "Perhaps the most important single thing a fly fisherman can know is the character and quality of the streams he fishes." All too often anglers arriving to fish western waters have not strategically planned for the success of their trip. But the character and quality of a stream are among the easiest things for an angler to learn, because so much has been written about most of our blue-ribbon streams.

I frequently see visiting fly fishermen show up in June to fish a particular stretch of the Yellowstone River—only to discover that that portion does not open to fishing until July 15. Or they show up in West Yellowstone in late July and complain that they have just spent two days on the Firehole River without taking a fish, unaware that the water temperature of the Firehole approaches 85 degrees at that time of the summer and will not cool to favorable trout temperatures again until late August. Many times during the season I hear of anglers who plan to fish the Madison in the morning and then drive to the Bighorn to drift hoppers in the afternoon.

When I ask where they'll be spending the night, they tell me they'll be returning to West Yellowstone, where they reserved a room. From West Yellowstone to the Bighorn River and back is a 700-mile round-trip.

Two things limit the success of the thousands of visiting anglers I talk to each season: trying to fish too much water in too little time, and a total lack of planning.

BEFORE YOU GO

Knowing the rivers, lakes, and streams you plan to fish can pay big dividends and save you time and money. Books such as Charlie Brooks's *Fishing Yellowstone Waters*, Howard Back's *The Waters of Yellowstone with Rod and Fly*, Chuck Fothergill's *Montana Fishing Guide*, and my and Clayton Molinero's *The Yellowstone Fly-Fishing Guide* contain valuable information, maps, and directions to most area waters. Brooks's *Nymph Fishing for Larger Trout* as well as my and John Juracek's *Fly Patterns of Yellowstone* and *Fishing Yellowstone Hatches* furnish accurate insect emergence dates, fly patterns, fishing techniques, the best times to visit, and pitfalls to avoid. Included in this book is a bibliography listing these and other works for further research on these subjects.

FLY SHOPS

Most fly shops offer reliable information; those that do not are short-lived. Keep in mind, however, that most shops in the West and especially in the Yellowstone area have a very limited business season. This means that during the off season, usually November through May, you can call and expect to get answers and advice from fly-shop personnel. When stopping by or calling the shops during the height of the business season, though, you will often have to wait in line or be put on hold. Do yourself and the fly shops a favor and call for trip-planning advice during the off season or well in advance of your trip.

When the shop owner gives advice, listen! Many times I give information and know it's falling on deaf ears. Excited anglers fire off question after question before I can even answer the first one. Relax and listen closely to the advice of experts in the area you plan to fish.

Many shops will gladly put together itineraries of places to fish during your stay. They will suggest flies you should tie to match emergences, recommend places to stay, provide car-rental information, suggest things for the nonfisherman to do while you are on the stream, name other fly shops to check with if you plan to move on to another area, and more.

If you ask, listen, and contact the fly shop during the off season or well in advance of your trip, the information you receive will go a long way toward a successful trip.

GUIDES

I wish Larry and I had taken advantage of a guide's services when I first fished Yellowstone waters 25 years ago. Instead, we drove around and fished a lot of unproductive waters with the wrong flies at the wrong times of day in the wrong types of weather. We'd try to fish tiny blue-winged olive mayflies on the Firehole on sunny, warm days instead of waiting for the rainy-snowy conditions optimal for this species' emergence. Or we'd drive across Yellowstone Park to fish the Lamar River after two days of rain, not realizing it would be too muddy to fish.

We were trying to save money, but we were also trying to save our egos. We'd read, listened to, and written for advice—and in fact did quite well considering that we were trying to fish too much water in too little time. Still, looking back on our trip, we figured almost half of it had been spent unproductively.

An experienced local guide is full of valuable information. He or she will know the area's waters and can pass that knowledge on to you. His or her fee is mostly for this information. Take a guide for a day or two and pick his brain for techniques, strategies, fly patterns, and insect emergences. Book the guide well in advance, and inform the fly shop or outfitter when you do so what you expect from him or her. Some guides specialize in certain techniques; others can take you to waters off the beaten path if that's what you want. Usually guides are booked for most of the season, so giving yours plenty of notice of your angling desires will allow him or her to check out some underfished, out-of-the-way waters before your arrival. Guides don't like to be surprised with a request to fish or check out "exotic" places on the day of the trip.

Experienced guides know the area's stream and lake entomology and enjoy explaining it to their clients. Most guides are innovative fly tiers, too, and are proud of their patterns. Often guided trips begin or end at the tying table, with the guide showing his client favorite patterns for the day or explaining a tying kink discussed on stream that day.

When booking a guided trip through a fly shop, ask to visit the water that will be fishing best at the general time of your scheduled trip; leave the specific day up to the guide. When arrangements haven't been made in advance and you simply show up at the shop or meet your guide on the river, tell your guide what type of fishing you want to do. But it's usually best to have the guide decide where to fish that day. Be open to his suggestions. A good guide will put you on the best water at the best time. He understands fly fishermen, hatches, fly patterns, weather, and wind; he is intimately familiar with trout and the streams they inhabit. He will usually know much more about the area's trout fishing than you do, and you can learn a great deal from him. He is there to make your day productive and enjoyable, and by listening and being courteous you can help him to do that. And remember to show your appreciation when your guide performs well. A standard gratuity is 15 to 25 percent. If a problem arises during the day, tell your guide about it and work things out. Guides are professionals and they expect to be treated accordingly.

OTHER SOURCES OF
INFORMATION FOR THE ANGLER

Most of our western waters flow through or lie on public lands. For information on these lands and waters, contact the agencies responsible for administering them. United States Forest Service and Bureau of Land Management (BLM) offices can provide maps and other information regarding the watersheds in their respective jurisdictions. Many forest service and BLM offices have staff biologists who can offer valuable information. Also, these agencies usually have information on other forms of recreation—hiking, birding, geology, and more—that might interest fishing as well as nonfishing members of your group. If everyone is doing something that pleases him, and the fishermen are successful, then the strategic planning for that trip was done right. The anglers don't have to worry about whether nonfishing companions are having a good time; they can get to know the waters and concentrate on the fishing.

Another great resource is United States Geological Survey quadrangle maps, which I guarantee save you time, money, and boot leather. These maps furnish accurate information to anglers looking for waters to explore, and most are detailed enough to show beaver ponds and sloughs. In fact, I've often wished they weren't so detailed.

The DeLorme Mapping Company (P.O. Box 298, Freeport, ME 04032) publishes statewide books of quadrangle maps covering Montana, Wyoming, Idaho, and other western states. Invaluable to the angler, these books show distances between watersheds; all highways, secondary roads, and trails; elevations; mountain ranges; and more. They are available nationwide in fly shops and bookstores.

Park rangers, state fish and game wardens, and biologists are also good sources of information. Some of the best where-to-fish advice on waters off the beaten path can also come from police officers, gas station owners, and restaurant employees.

Recently the Internet has become a valuable resource for anglers. While some of the information is suspect, overall it is getting more accurate as quality fly shops and outfitters come on line—and most of the Internet's inaccurate information is simply grousing from dissatisfied anglers who failed to plan strategically for the success of their trips. The Internet is now furnishing information on rivers, lakes, and streams; when and where to fish; fly patterns; guides and outfitters; fly shops; gear; fly-tying materials; rental cars; airlines; and more.

CHAPTER 2

The Tools—
Equipment and Tackle

N o matter how good your fishing gear is, it cannot take the place of positive attitude, desire, concentration, skills, and knowledge from time on the water. Fly fishers who come West loaded with enthusiasm, desire, and a positive attitude are well on their way to having a fine trip. A willingness to learn new techniques and strategies, and practice them, is paramount. So is knowing your equipment, its limitations, and your own.

Concentration on the fishing at hand is important. Almost any veteran angler who has a bad day will explain that he "failed to concentrate."

Putting in your time and learning from experience on stream is imperative to success no matter where you fish.

Your physical preparedness is important, too. If you want to hike in to an alpine lake you'd better be in shape. Starting at an elevation of nearly 7,000 feet and hiking to a lake at 10,000 feet requires real physical effort. Wading and walking miles of stream can tax heart and lungs, as well. If you're serious about your western angling experiences, know your limits and get in serious physical shape.

As for the equipment itself, ask a hundred successful western anglers for their thoughts on gear and you'll get several hundred answers, most of them valid. So let's look at equipment: rods, reels, lines, wading gear, and the rest of the stuff anglers fuss over.

FLY RODS

I use a 9-foot, 4-weight Winston rod for most of my dry-fly fishing during the summer. I prefer a slow-action graphite that forces me to slow down between presentations and concentrate on the float of the fly, the rises of the fish, the insects on the water, and the emergence stage the fish are working. The slower-action graphite also protects fine tippets. The Sage LL (Lightline), Thomas & Thomas Paradigm, and Orvis Western Spring Creek rods also have the slow graphite feel I prefer for summer dry-fly fishing. For lake angling, early- and late-season streamers, large nymphs, big bushy salmonflies, or hoppers on big water such as the Yellowstone, I prefer a 9-foot, 7-weight Sage SP rod fished with a 6-weight double-taper line. This helps me defeat heavy afternoon western winds, and also allows me to pick my line and fly off the water and make my next cast, usually without false casting. When I'm using big flies in heavy winds or have to pick a lot of line off the water quickly to get back to moving trout without false casting, I prefer a fast-action rod with plenty of backbone. Orvis HLS[2] and Winston LT rods are fine tools for this type of angling.

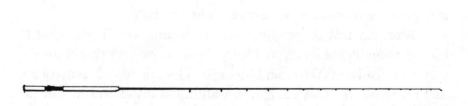

FIGURE 1 – SPEY ROD VS. CONVENTIONAL FLY ROD

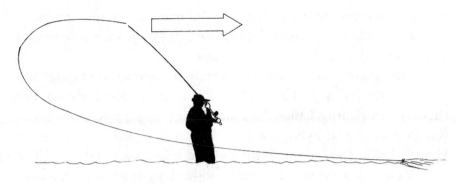

FIGURE 2 – DEMONSTRATION OF THE SINGLE SPEY CAST

Spey rods are becoming popular among anglers who fish big water during our fall runs of brown and rainbow trout. The beauty of learning to fish with the spey is that you can present a continuous fixed-length cast to holding water without stripping in line and false casting to get back to the holds. Spey rods are invaluable for reaching water where bankside trees or other obstructions make a backcast impossible. While the rods are heavy—sometimes ungainly —and presentation with them might not be considered "delicate," they are finding a place in western angling. Look for the spey rod to catch on even more among serious anglers for fall fishing.

FLY REELS

Walk into any well-stocked western fly shop and you will be faced with nearly as many fly-reel choices as fly patterns. For stream angling in Yellowstone country I prefer the simple single-action, click-drag, lightweight reels that have been around for decades. My favorites are the Hardy Lightweight series and Orvis CFO series. Both provide a reliable light-drag system that protects fine tippets and light-wire hooks yet is strong enough to subdue wild rainbow and brown trout in the currents of the Madison or Yellowstone River. The reel should also be large enough to hold 50 yards of 20-pound-test backing. One of the benefits of modern catch-and-release and progressive fishing regulations is the increased average size of trout.

In my stream-fishing log I have recorded being taken into my backing on the Madison, Henry's Fork, and Yellowstone more than a dozen times during the last three seasons.

Lake anglers require reels with smooth light to stout drags and the capacity for up to 100 yards of 20- or 30-pound backing. For this type of fishing I like the Lamson (by Sage) and Abel reels. Rainbow-cutthroat hybrids of 8 to 15 pounds are taken regularly on Henry's Lake, and gulping rainbows and browns on Hebgen, Cliff, and Wade Lakes average 17 inches, so backing is a must. One note here is that cruising gulpers must often be cast to at considerable distances. These fish are moving, never stationary, unlike river fish. Fifty- to 70-foot casts are common, and a trout needs only a short run from there to get into your backing. Here a smooth drag is a must to protect fine tippets and small light-wire hooks. Last summer my lake-fishing companion Phil Takatsuno and I were into our backing at least once every time we fished together.

You can expect to get what you pay for in a reel and rod, so get the best you can afford. Practice and get to know both tools. Develop your skills with them so that when the fish of your trip is hooked you know just how much pressure you can put on him, and just how much backing you have on your reel.

WADING GEAR

For wading rivers such as the Madison during most of the season I prefer the new microfiber stocking-foot wader, either waist or chest high, available from almost every wader manufacturer. This fine product is lightweight and has a neoprene foot, which adds warmth for cold-water wading. I no longer wet-wade, and neither would you if you had seen my leg after it was bitten by a water beetle a few years back. The microfiber wader is also good for float tubing during the warm months.

With these waders I use the best felt wading shoes available. There are two to pick from: the River Gripper by the Danner Boot Company, and the Simms Plastek boot. An orthopedic surgeon diagnosed a foot problem I have and he gave me a choice: Use the finest wading shoe available or have corrective surgery. Both of these brands of shoes offer fine support and protection, and they feel great.

During the cold months of October through April I usually go with boot-foot neoprene waders for their insulating qualities. They're also easy getting into and out of. I have spent too much time dancing around the back of pickup trucks trying to get into a stocking-foot wader, then wading booties, and finally wading shoes while the snow or cold rain dampened my socks and pants. I own two pair of boot-foot waders: some Simms full neoprenes with boot feet that I cannot seem to wear out even after six seasons, and my newest waders, Orvis microfibers with neoprene-lined boot feet, which I wore all last spring and fall. The Orvis pair is lightweight and easier to get into and out of, but when it's really cold I prefer the full neoprenes.

I do own a pair of hip boots, which I love to wear. But there are so few places I can do so without getting a bootful of water once or twice a day that they seldom see service.

For anglers not used to the slippery boulders and heavy currents of many of our western rivers I recommend a wading staff.

VEST VERSUS PACK

I spend a fair amount of time hiking and searching for underfished and overlooked waters in the backcountry. When doing so I prefer to wear Patagonia's vest-backpack combination; I find I use this now for over half of my time on stream. The vest holds my fishing tackle, while the pack has room for my rain gear, cameras, lunch, water bottle, and so on. When I'm not using the vest-backpack combination for hiking in to fishing spots, I wear a Simms Master Vest.

For lake fishing, whether in a float tube or boat, I go with a pack. There are several on the market today and I haven't yet found one I don't like, as long as it has the capacity to hold fly boxes, floatant, tippets, bug dope, sunscreen, and the like. My favorite is the Patagonia Hip Chest Pack.

HATS AND EYEWEAR

A hat or visor with a dark brim underside is required for sight fishing as well as shading when you're searching into the sun for rising trout. I prefer one with a long bill, like the kind Ernest Hemingway wore. Such a hat not only keeps the sun's rays from causing problems when I'm searching for rising trout or trying to locate them holding in the current but also keeps rain and snow off my glasses.

I carry two sunglass-lens colors when fishing. The one I wear most is brown—polarized, of course—which is best on bright days. The other is amber, which I wear on overcast days or when fishing early or late. I once tried gray lenses, which I had heard were great on dark days. Toward the end of the afternoon a snowstorm crept in over the Continental Divide and started dumping huge wet flakes on the Baker's Hole stretch of the Madison River above Hebgen Lake. The spawning browns and tag-along fall rainbows became active as the light got dimmer, making it tough to see. I finally had to remove my glasses to thread on a fresh Light Spruce streamer to replace the one broken off by a big hook-jawed male rainbow that jumped four times trying to free the fly from his jaw. I promised myself only a few more casts before calling it a day. Even now, 12 years later, I can see that next false cast coming back at me in the wind, carrying the #2 fly toward my eye. I ducked too late and it penetrated my left eyelid. Water and blood ran into my eye and down my cheek, and I knew I had lost my dominant eye. Panic set in as I made my way back to the car, holding the leader and keeping the tension off the fly. I was certain I had punctured my eyeball. Just then my friend Bob Hoar came around the bend and saw my predicament. I was explaining that the hook was barbless just as he backed the fly out of my eyelid. Luckily, the hook had only scratched my eye, not penetrated. I got rid of the gray-lens glasses the next day.

LANDING NET

I do not carry a net. I fish barbless, and when I get my trout within reach I take my forceps, clamp them onto the hook, and work it free. One hand brings the trout near by guiding him in with the tippet, while the other releases him via the forceps. I seldom touch a trout as I release him.

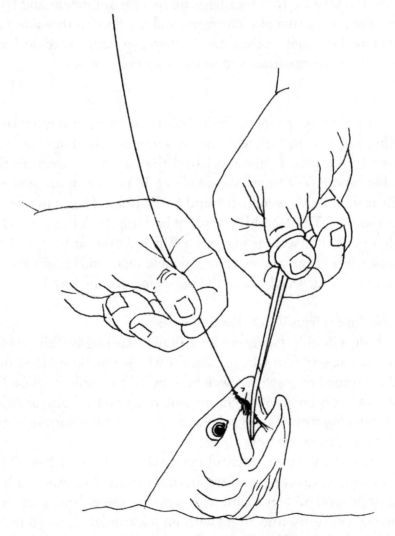

FIGURE 3 – CATCHING AND RELEASING A TROUT WITHOUT A NET

TACKLE

Fly fishing western waters successfully requires a wide variety of fly-fishing strategies. Our unique and varied water types, big and wild trout, changing weather conditions, and strong afternoon winds require special leader-tippet configurations and shock absorption; special fly patterns; sinking and floating double-taper and weight-forward as well as dyed fly lines; the fishing of tandem and triple flies, often using nymphs, emergers, and dry flies on the same cast; and more. Let's look at these tackle strategies designed to deal with the challenging situations our western waters present.

FLY LINES

The fly line is one of the foundations successful western fly fishing is built on, yet few anglers know much about fly lines. When I visit with fishermen I find that most are unaware that double-taper (DT) lines take up about 30 percent more space on their reels than do weight-forward (WF) lines. They can't understand why a DT line and 100 yards of backing won't fit on a reel for which the manufacturer suggests a WF and 100 yards of backing. Most anglers are also unaware that double-taper and weight-forward lines of the same weight have the same taper for the first 30 feet.

Double-Taper versus Weight-Forward Lines

I use a double-taper line for all my fly fishing in Yellowstone, with the exception of lake fishing, for which I use a sinking line—and am forced to go with a weight-forward line only because DTs have not yet been produced in the sink rate I prefer. I also use a WF for fishing big nymphs and streamers on or near the bottom, which we'll look into in the next chapter.

Still, the great majority of my casting is done within 30 feet on streams, or to rising, cruising trout on stillwaters. And if I have to cast beyond 30 feet I can, with a double-taper line, pick more than 30 feet of fly line along with an additional 12 to 18 feet of leader and tippet off the water, due to the line's weight and taper.

And such long-line pickups can be the rule when fishing to cruis-ing trout on lakes. With a weight-forward line I usually have to strip in the running line, which comes after the initial taper, to get to the heavier taper before I can pick the line off the water. If the trout are cruising, frustration is often the result.

Stream Angling: Floating versus Sinking Lines

I have tied my feet together and dislodged many underwater boulders, separated fly-line coating from its core, and more—all while trying to use sinking lines in western rivers and streams. Many anglers tell me that they can fish effectively with sinking lines in our rivers, but when I join them on the water I note that they, too, have many of these same problems. I have much more success using standard double-taper fly lines and a short fast-taper leader with weight in the fly or on the leader to get a fly down to the bottom.

DYED FLY LINES

Before I nail-knot my line to the backing I dye it an olive color. The dyeing process makes the line limp and supple, which increases its castability. Also, I have had many trout rise near a brightly colored line, only to spook and bolt when they saw or touched it. A dyed line more closely approximates aquatic or streamside vegetation, and I've noticed far less line detection by the trout. On several occasions while fishing a bright line on Hebgen, Wade, or Yellowstone Lake, I've watched trout taking *Callibaetis* mayflies on the surface. Upon swim-ming up to or crossing closely under a bright line, each fish goes under and quits feeding. With a dyed line, however, I've watched trout take naturals and artificials at that line, cross under it, and even bump it without knowing it was there.

On spring creeks, casts are often made over weed beds, along banks laden with vegetation, and among drifting weeds. I've found dyed-olive lines to be essential for effective presentations.

I've tried white lines when there's snow on streambanks, and blue-dyed lines for clear, sunny conditions. Neither seems to work any bet-ter than the olive-dyed kind.

In currents, sinking fly lines tend to be buoyed by their bulk. Full-sinking lines become hooked on rocks and are always under-foot; they are also harder to cast, control, and mend. Even sink-tip lines cause problems, because the tip is often thrust to the surface by the current.

Backing

Because DT lines take up more space than WFs, I use less backing with them. I nail-knot the fly line to the backing with a five-turn knot and wind the line onto the spool. I look at hundreds of other anglers' reels during the course of the season and find that one of the biggest problems is too much backing on the reel spool. This causes binding, forcing the fly line against the reel frame and damaging it. You may also have this problem if you allow a shop to put backing and line on your reel with a machine. Such machines are too efficient: They put on line so evenly and tightly that no fisherman can rewind it as nicely. The results are maddening: binding lines on frames. I never use a machine to load lines, and I always leave about 3/8-inch between my line and the frame supports to prevent binding and line damage.

LEADERS, "GUM," AND TIPPETS

Walk into any fly shop in the world today and you will be greeted by a wall of leaders and tippets. Even though dozens of choices make it seem complicated, it is not.

For most of my fishing I start with a 9-foot knotless leader tapered down to 4X tippet. If I'm fishing a 6-weight rod, I use a .023 leader butt. On my 4-weight rod a .021 butt section is my choice.

I tie a proper nail knot to connect the leader to the fly line, using a small tying tool designed for the purpose. When I demonstrate this technique for an angler at the shop, I often find that he is surprised at how easy it is to tie a good nail knot with a tool. A three- or four-turn nail knot tied properly creates a better connection between line and leader than even the best splice.

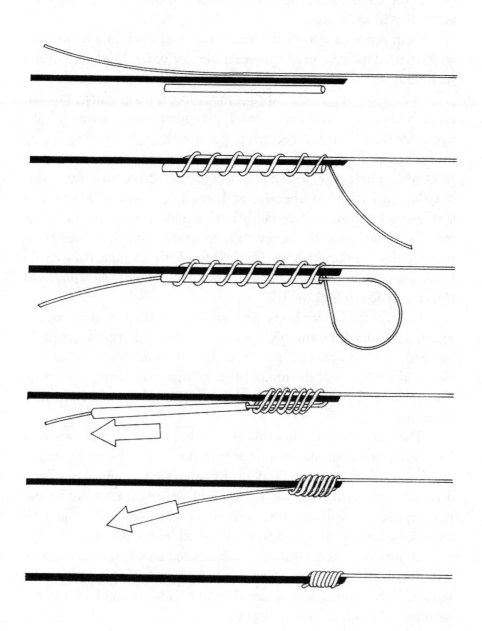

FIGURE 4 – NAIL KNOT

After knotting on the leader, I follow it down 36 to 42 inches and splice in some gum.

Gum is not new to fly fishing. It's been around for a while, and western anglers have used it successfully for years. Marketed under such names as *shock gum*, *high power gum*, and simply *power gum*, it is a shock-absorbing material that looks like monofilament but has enough elasticity to prevent break-offs when you're using a light tippet for big fish. It has become popular with anglers fishing spring creeks and stillwaters, and even on fast-current rivers such as the Madison, where the fish have become selective to tiny *Baetis* mayflies, microcaddis species, and small terrestrials. Masters of spring-creek fishing such as Herbert Wellington use gum, and it has made a tremendous difference in their ability to catch huge trout on tiny dry flies and 6X to 7X tippets. Without gum they could hook but seldom land larger trout, due to the fragility of the light tippets needed to fool the fish.

I've watched Herb hook and land brown trout over 28 inches long on #16 dry flies and 6X tippets with the aid of power gum in his leaders. It absorbs the initial shock of the take, the bolting run, the head jerking, and the jumps of such large trout while protecting the tippet and preventing the light-wire hook from bending or breaking.

The only drawback to using gum is that you must learn another knot with which to incorporate it into the leader. But the double-jam knot is easy to learn, and after you've tied it a few times and used it to successfully hook and land big trout on tiny hooks and light tippets you will never be without gum in your leaders again. It has allowed many an angler to land the fish of his lifetime.

So now we have a 9-foot leader tapered to 4X, with a splice of 6 to 8 inches of power gum included. As a general rule, this leader setup will work fine for most dry-fly and standard nymph situations, with the addition of proper tippets.

I feel strongly that long, fine leaders are required for most dry-fly situations on our waters. Many anglers still believe that angling

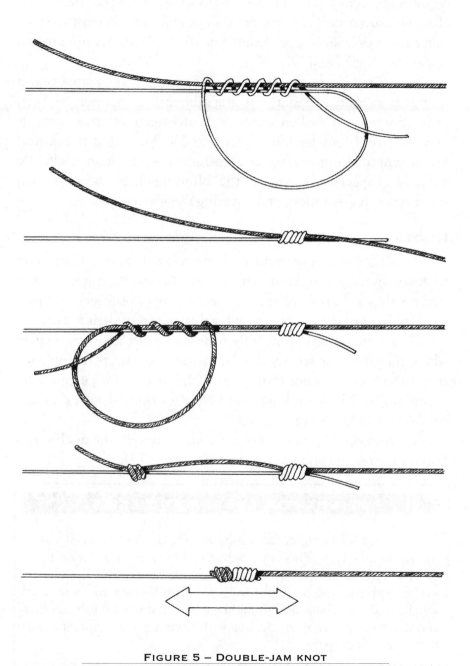

FIGURE 5 – DOUBLE-JAM KNOT

requires less delicacy in the West than in other areas of the world. However, successfully fishing dry flies or emergers on most western water requires leader-tippet lengths of 16 to 18 feet, terminating in tippets of 5X, 6X, and 7X.

Of course, there are situations for which heavier tippets and shorter leaders are necessary. Fishing salmonflies, Mormon crickets, or big hoppers on broken water or during fierce afternoon winds may require 9-foot leaders tapered to 3X. Matching tippet and leader lengths to individual circumstances is a book in itself. We will look at specialized setups in the following chapter as we discuss water types, presentation, and covering the water.

KNOTS

Knots are very important to anglers, but most fishermen tend to learn more about knots than they do about strategies, the streams they fish, the emergences and behavior of insects, fly patterns, presentation, and planning for the success of their fishing.

There are only two knots fly fishermen must know, no matter where they fish; one secures the fly, the other connects the tippet. I still prefer a clinch knot or improved clinch knot for putting a fly on my tippet. The knot I use exclusively for tippet-leader connections is a double surgeon's knot.

I recommend learning two other knots as well: the double-jam knot (see page 21) and the nail knot (see page 19).

WEIGHTS ON LEADER AND FLIES

The use of lead weights for fishing is forbidden by law in all waters in Yellowstone Park. This law is scheduled to be extended soon to all trout waters in the United States. A nonlead, removable sinker is available; please use it. As for weight within fly patterns, a no-lead weight is also available and should be used. I'll discuss weight on flies and leaders in the chapters dealing with covering water types, presentation, and fly patterns.

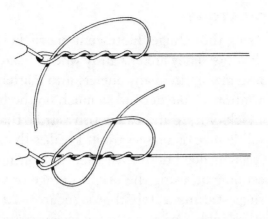

FIGURE 6 – IMPROVED CLINCH KNOT

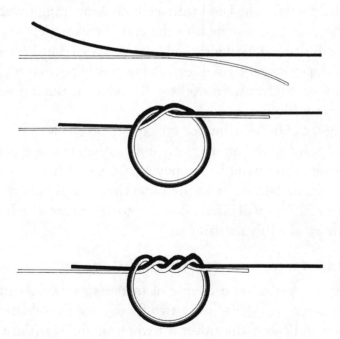

FIGURE 7 – SURGEON'S KNOT

STRIKE INDICATORS

I dislike using those huge fluorescent plastic bobbers referred to as strike indicators. They are unsightly when discarded along the waters. They also mesmerize many anglers into inattentiveness or a loss of concentration. Some depend so much on the bobber's overt movement, or lack of it, to indicate a fish's strike that they fail to see the more subtle take of a larger trout. I realize that some anglers with failing eyesight need help with their nymphing. This is the only time I recommend using the bright orange or yellow plastic indicators. I suggest using a style that is securely attached to the leader with either rubber or a toothpick because these remain on your leader and will not become litter.

For anglers who do not need bright plastic, I always recommend using a big dry fly for an indicator. Simply tie additional tippet to the dry fly at the bend with a clinch knot or improved clinch knot, then knot your nymph to the end of this tippet. The tippet length will depend on depth and current speed, but I have never fished a tippet longer than 4 feet. A big grasshopper or cricket, dry salmonfly, or Wulff pattern works well, and many times trout rise to the indicator itself.

When caddis, mayflies, or midges are on the water I often go with a crippled adult pattern as my indicator and tie a tippet with a trailing emerger, nymph, or pupa pattern. When caddis and mayflies are on the water at the same time you should try imitations of each. This will often allow you to determine which stage or which insect the fish are rising to.

SPECIAL TWO- AND THREE-FLY SETUPS

We just looked at a couple of instances in western angling where it can be helpful to use a two-fly rig: one fly a floating, visible strike indicator, the other a nymph or surface-film pattern, which is difficult or impossible for anglers to see.

But there are other times when two- and three-fly casts should be incorporated into your strategy. In cases of salmonfly activity, brown trout often concentrate on nymphs at the shoreline while

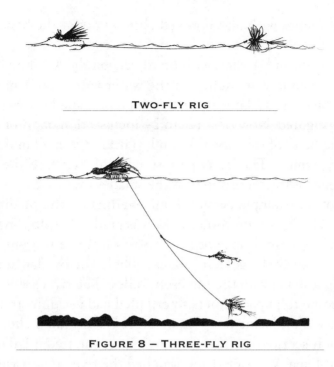

TWO-FLY RIG

FIGURE 8 – THREE-FLY RIG

rainbows prefer adults along the banks and in pockets and runs near shore. Here, use a nymph and an adult in tandem, casting to all likely looking holds. Browns usually take subsurface flies, while rainbows feed on top.

On stillwaters, fish may take the same fly at different depths, according to the life cycle of the insect. For example, on Grebe Lake in Yellowstone Park both grayling and rainbow trout relish damselflies. Unweighted nymph patterns fished in the surface film usually entice rainbows, whereas weighted flies take grayling during the same hatch. Many times you will be rewarded with two fish on the same cast—one a grayling, the other a wild rainbow.

On lakes where *Callibaetis* mayflies are active, a three-fly cast is preferable at times. Here, your first fly should be a crippled dun, your second an unweighted nymph imitating the unwinged insect at the moment it is attempting to emerge into a dun. Finally, your bottom fly should be a weighted nymph that imitates a natural migrating to the surface to emerge. Tie each pattern to a tippet of about 18 inches with an improved clinch knot at the bend of the fly above it.

On rivers and streams with no insects on the water and no rising trout visible, you might fish the water with a tandem nymph setup. A favorite is a large stonefly nymph or cranefly larva pattern, heavily weighted. Now tie a 12- to 24-inch section of 3X or 4X tippet to the bend of the larger fly, and to it knot a small midge larva or mayfly nymph. The larger pattern not only serves as the weight but also may attract a fish to it or the smaller fly.

Another example occurred one evening on the Madison last summer. The harsh afternoon light was gradually softening as the Gravelly Mountain Range began to feast on the setting sun's burning edges. Slowly the golden ball was gobbled up by Flat Iron Peak, spreading a shadow up the Madison Valley. The river's trout began to rise, some to pupae, others to crippled caddis adults trapped in the surface film. Jackie first tied on an X Caddis, then clinched on an 18-inch section of 5X tippet, to which she tied a LaFontaine Emergent Pupa. We waited and watched the river and its wild trout from our perch atop a boulder impaled on the bank where a tiny spring entered the main stream. First, smaller trout launched themselves out of the water, rising to emerging *Hydropsyche* caddis. Shortly, the larger fish began working, their tails and dorsal fins barely breaking the surface as they fed in the calm, shallow water next to shore. Jackie allowed the larger trout to rise several times so they could become confident and establish a deliberate rhythm before she presented her first cast to them. The first trout preferred the pupa to the crippled adult. After that, most of the rising fish were taken on the more visible X Caddis, which doubled as a strike indicator. We fished the pool until 11 P.M. when we finally left the rising trout to head in for a late dinner. Five o'clock and work were but a short sleep away.

There are no hard-and-fast rules or techniques for using two- and three-fly casts. Be innovative and flexible. Try different patterns, tippet lengths, and presentations on varied waters for success. Find what works for you.

PART TWO

The
Skills

CHAPTER 3

Reading
Western Waters

W hile it's impossible for you to get to know everything
about the streams you plan to fish in Yellowstone country, there are many books and videos available that can eliminate
much of the guesswork. Knowing the water types and how to read
them are two big pieces you must fit together to solve the western-
angling puzzle.

I often see anglers fishing every inch of a stream, whether it
could possibly hold trout or not. Just last summer Jackie and I
fished across the Madison River from four anglers who never
moved from an area the size of a tennis court. For five hours they
looked like a group of marionettes performing on the river. Later
that afternoon we ran into them in the parking lot at the Cliff and
Wade Lakes bridge. They asked if we had fished that day, and we
said we'd done well fishing a pale morning mayfly emergence near
the West Fork. Their response was that they hadn't seen a mayfly
all day. They had taken a few whitefish on Prince Nymphs, but no
trout, even though they had fished the same area we had. They
went on to tell us that they were just starting out in fly fishing and

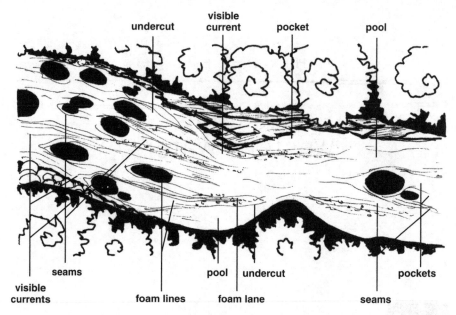

FIGURE 9 – A TYPICAL HEAVY-WATER RIVER

could use all the help they could get; they'd fished the "chuck-and-chance" method for four days and had yet to take a trout. One of them said, "Where we're from, we would've taken several trout in four days." Turns out that at home they fish for trout planted weekly in water too warm to support a year-round population; the planting is only successful during the coldest weeks of the year. To catch trout at home these anglers didn't have to read the water. They simply had to fish where the truck dumped in the fish.

Here in Yellowstone country we are fortunate to have so much quality water that sustains wild trout. Our streams are not stocked. We're also fortunate to have so many water types to explore and learn to read and fish successfully. Each type requires different fly-fishing strategies.

Nearly all western rivers and streams have more than one water type. The Henry's Fork, for instance, is a huge, gently flowing spring creek with smooth, even currents in the Railroad Ranch stretch, just downstream from Last Chance, Idaho; a mile upstream it becomes a noisy, heavy, swift torrent churning through Box Canyon. Large, boulder-strewn riffle-and-pocket-water rivers such as Montana's Madison have many microhabitats along their lengths. For example, during the month of May on one short stretch of the Madison anglers must be prepared to match a spring-creek-like emergence of #22 *Baetis* mayfly duns. At the same time, 50 yards upstream trout are feasting on such classic freestone inhabitants as giant stonefly nymphs migrating to shore in preparation for hatching in June.

It's a mistake to classify an entire river or stream as one specific water type and use a single strategy to fish it all. As you move around on a river, or from one river to the next, you must be flexible, alert, and ready and willing to switch tactics with each stream's changing water type. Also, changing seasons, weather conditions, time of day, insect emergences, and desired methods of fishing can affect water type, the way you read it, and effective strategy. Reading western water correctly is the first step in locating trout and preparing to raise them to your fly.

THE HEAVY-WATER STRETCHES

In 1959 an earthquake collapsed a mountainside and sent more than 80 million tons of rock across the Madison River, damming it and creating Earthquake Lake. Now, during the high-water days of June, the Madison rips out of Hebgen Dam and mixes with the torrential, muddied Cabin and Beaver Creeks. Locals sometimes gather to watch the spectacle of the river taking out the natural dam forming Earthquake Lake. Boulders the size of earthmovers, snags, and a few live trees that are barely making a go of it on the near-barren moonscape left by the devastating quake come crashing down into the Madison gorge. The river undercuts and eats its way through the natural dam each high-water spring.

During the 1989 spring runoff Dick McGuire, who has guided, fished, and lived on the river since the early 1930s and knows it better than anyone, pointed out to us a waterfall moving upstream.

The water was eating away at the riverbed, and the waterfall was actually moving upstream as the currents chewed the bottom out. Suddenly, one of the earthmover-sized rocks crashed down from its undermined position atop the river's channel and blocked the current on the riverbed, shutting down the moving waterfall temporarily. Earthquake Lake is on borrowed time; the earthen dam is further eroded every spring. One day the river will breach nature's dam permanently and the once-great section of river currently impounded in Earthquake Lake will be a heavy, rumbling river again.

Western rivers and streams flowing through canyons or gorges are typically heavy waters. They rumble noisily over slick, boulder-strewn stretches or jagged lava rocks, creating seams, foam lines, feeding lanes, pockets, pools, and more. All are features characteristic of heavy water. Waters such as the Madison River from Hebgen Dam downstream to the town of Three Forks, the Gallatin River, the Box Canyon stretch of the Henry's Fork River, and the gorge between the first meadow and the campground on Slough Creek are examples of heavy waters.

Heavy waters are often hard or impossible to wade, and they're always dangerous. Usually they're rich in insect life. These waters are difficult to read for anglers first experiencing them. I can recall many anglers new to the West complaining that they had fished for several days on the heavy waters and failed to take a decent-sized trout. I also know local anglers who refuse to learn this water type.

Our heavy waters change during the course of the seasons. An example is the Madison below Hebgen Dam. One of my friends complained that he had tried it in October and the same water had not fished as well as it had during July. I explained that in July the river runs at around 1,000 cubic feet per second, but in October the Montana Power Company begins to draw the lake down to capture the next spring's snowmelt. The river runs from 1,500 to almost 2,000 cubic feet per second during the late drawdown, from September through November. "No wonder I had a hard time wading the river," my friend said. "I could barely get out to the runs I fished in July. When I did get to them I couldn't bump bottom with my nymphs, even with three split shot on."

Trout do not occupy every inch of water in a river, especially not in a heavy-flowing one. Western trout will not move far for a fly, natural or artificial. Obviously, it's critical to fish the holding water, where the trout are and where they're accustomed to getting their food.

To me, heavy water is the easiest of all water types to read and learn because it offers lots of clues. There are its visible currents, foam lines, pockets, seams, undercuts, and obstructions such as boulders and logs. And the noise of the current allows you to get close to the holding water.

Visible currents are just that. The water moves swiftly around rocks and over falls, whirlpooling and bubbling behind downed timber. Or it appears as white water atop a boulder when heavy currents leave a standing wave.

Visible currents, and relief from these currents, mean trout are present in size and number. The three items most required by stream fish are safety from predators, food, and relief from heavy currents. Our heavy rivers offer many obstructions that provide such relief. These obstructions, including boulders and logjams, also provide security and food sources.

Pockets, foam lines, and undercuts are the next features to look for while fishing heavy water. A **pocket** is smooth, usually deep water located below a boulder, logjam, or beaver lodge. Fish often use pocket water on the Madison for feeding, security, and relief from the current. But as rivers such as the Madison receive more angling pressure, trout have begun to avoid some of the productive pockets along the shorelines during daylight—moving into them to hold and feed only in the late evening and early morning.

Foam lanes are obvious but seldom recognized as providers of food and escape routes for fish. Thin **foam lines** are found along boulder-strewn banks where several currents merge. They appear directly behind or immediately next to boulders in the main currents and are associated with visible currents. The foam line then spreads out, usually at about the point where trout begin to use it for holding and feeding, in the broader, slower currents and becomes a **foam lane**. Generally, lanes must be 6 inches or more wide before trout will use them for security, food, and relief from heavier currents.

Seams are perhaps the hardest features of all for anglers to read. A **seam** is the margin between water too heavy for trout to hold, feed, and feel secure in and water too shallow to provide these important features. Seams are the transition water that trout often prefer to hold in, particularly in turbulent areas of a river. The best Yellowstone-country fly fishermen say that seams are more often "felt" than read. Some seams are "hard": The water that separates the inside quiet water from the outside fast water on the sides and rear of a boulder, for example, is a hard seam. There are seams on and beneath the surface, and they are also associated with visible currents, foam lanes, pockets, undercuts, and obstructions. As you put in your time on our waters, you'll come to know and recognize more productive seams with each trip. They produce more quality trout than any other area.

To be successful you must be able to locate holding water in all water types. Holding water is the trout's living room and usually its kitchen, too. It affords the fish protection and food. It also offers a security area—one that the trout can use to temporarily avoid anglers as they fish, walk, wade, or float through its holding area.

In the past, we saw fish scurry away and hide for hours upon our incautious approach to the stream. But angling pressure has increased during the past several years, and trout in heavily fished waters have adapted. They have to feed when the water temperature is optimal, or they will suffer. Now, a trout knowing of or at times sensing an angler's presence sneaks off to a submerged log, rock, or undercut to avoid the angler. Once the angler passes by or quits casting to the fish, the trout will immediately come out of hiding or begin rising in his holding water again. Sometimes he will circle a wading angler, take up a position downstream, and begin feeding off what the angler is kicking up. This is common on sections of smooth-flowing rivers such as the Yellowstone, where scores of fishermen work the cutthroats that cruise from wader to wader. But on heavy water such as the Madison, along with heavily fished spring creeks, this is new behavior.

Another "new trout" we have come to note in our heavy-water stretches is the one that moves to shallow water to escape fishing pressure. These fish have begun to take up less obvious holding waters to avoid floating and wading anglers. This water has thus become important to anglers who are seeking the challenge of sight fishing for larger fish, and who are willing to spend time carefully walking the banks and searching, rather than wading and casting to obvious holding water. Usually such anglers must "settle for" far fewer but larger trout than the typical fisherman. On blue-ribbon rivers such as the Madison there are so many wild trout per mile that you simply need a bit of faith, patience, concentration, and a pair of polarized sunglasses to be rewarded with many fine trout in the slow, thin margins of water only 6 to 12 inches deep. Here you will actually see the trout—often a tail or dorsal fin—as it cruises, searching for food. But you must be careful here, too: Often a trout will lie stationary, and all that you'll see is a glint of tail or nose as the fish rests in the shallows or takes a mayfly emerger or leafhopper in the surface film.

SMOOTH, EVEN WATERS

Smooth waters are characterized by easy, even, smooth currents, often interspersed with riffles, runs, glides, and pools. This water type often includes sections of heavy canyon water but more typical is a meadow stream with meanders, undercuts, grazing bison and elk, great emergences of caddis and mayflies, fine terrestrial angling, and lovely rising wild trout. Examples of smooth water are Slough and Pelican Creeks, and the Lamar and Upper Yellowstone Rivers from the upper falls to Yellowstone Lake.

You will find this water easily readable, although not without its surprises at times. Usually the surprises are pleasant—large wild trout barely leaving a dimple as they sip minute mayfly spinners in the surface film, or slashing rises sending sprays of water onto the streamside grasses as fish attack gargantuan Mormon crickets. These crickets are each about the size of a 1/4-pound hamburger. They begin their late-summer migration for mating and egg-laying purposes on the dry grass benches above the smooth meadow streams.

Reading smooth water requires patience, concentration, bank walking, good eyesight, and plenty of bug spray to keep away the July snipe flies. One problem you might experience on smooth waters such as the Lamar River, or the Yellowstone River near Buffalo Ford, is fish migration. An area that produces one day can be void of fish the next.

Fisheries biologist Lynn Kaeding of the U.S. Fish and Wildlife Service in Yellowstone National Park reports that it is not uncommon for cutthroat trout to migrate between Yellowstone Lake and the Buffalo Ford picnic area on the Yellowstone River, an area of 6 to 8 miles, in a day or less. Tagged cutthroats have been tracked on their migrations in and out of the lake on several occasions. Several trout implanted with radio transmitters turned up missing a few summers back. Just after they passed a checkpoint midway between Buffalo Ford and the lake, their transmitters failed. One biologist in the study group suggested that they check out Frank Island on Yellowstone Lake, an area inhabited by pelicans. As they approached the island, their receiver began picking up transmitter signals from the missing trout again. It seems that pelicans had ingested the transmitters when they ate radio-tagged cutthroats, and then defecated them.

The entire length of the smooth-flowing Lamar River hosts tremendous migrations of fish on several occasions during the season. It is believed that summer thunderstorms, which can cause extreme fluctuations in the river's flow, also cause changes in holding areas—perhaps explaining the migrations. The fish never adopt permanent holding areas as they do in streams with a more constant, stable flow. On the Lamar it pays to move a lot to locate trout, especially if the fish you found in a holding area one day are gone the next.

Reading smooth water means you should check the undercuts at meanders, weed banks, areas of overhanging vegetation, and banks at whose bases the river has gouged deep holes. Check out the riffles, deeper pools, and glides that run from pool to pool in streams such as Slough Creek and parts of the Lamar.

Four features found on smooth water are of extreme importance to fly fishers because they often concentrate insects and rising trout. Watch for whirlpools and their back currents, along with scum lines and feeding troughs. **Whirlpools** are formed when currents sweep around wing dams, sweepers, islands, and sloughed-off stream banks. At the ends of these features there are usually small, whirling **back currents** that collect insects. In such back currents and small whirlpools you can often locate a single trout or even whole pods that will rise to insect emergences or a properly presented terrestrial imitation. Because of the direction of flow in back currents and whirlpools, the trout may seem to be facing downstream. In fact, they're facing into the currents of these features as they swirl. Be alert.

Scum lines and **feeding troughs** are found when currents merge. Slough Creek, for instance, holds many areas where one current sweeps along an overhanging bank and another, coming off a gravel ledge, joins it. Here, cutthroats and rainbows feel secure holding in scum lines. When rising in these tight lines, trout will seldom move to take a fly. The naturals are being delivered to them in very narrow lanes, and the trout are so focused on the lane that they may never move even an inch to take a natural—or an artificial. In such spots trout may also drop back to where two lanes converge, forming the longer and wider lanes called feeding troughs. It's common on the upper meadows of Slough Creek to locate feeding troughs that form as currents merge from overhangs, undercuts, islands, and whirlpools. These feeding areas might be several yards long and several feet wide, and they may hold dozens of rising trout.

Big, smooth waters such as the Yellowstone can be a bit tougher to read because they are so large and apparently nondescript. Walk a bit of high bank, though, or drive along slowly and search for rising trout, and you will learn the Yellowstone well. Here the trout can be found holding just off the banks, in pools formed behind big chunks of lava rock, behind sweepers created by downed lodgepole and subalpine fir trees, near rock ledges, or atop and next to weed banks.

Yellowstone country's smooth water is some of the most pleasant you'll ever fish. With grand emergences of mayflies and caddis and wonderful terrestrial fishing during the late summer, you'll have plenty of rising trout to fish to. By studying this water type you can experience the ultimate in dry-fly angling.

SPRING CREEKS, LARGE AND SMALL

Without question, spring creeks offer the most challenging angling. Spring creeks mean selective trout rising to one of the many phases of an insect emergence. These creeks feature clear water that flows smoothly in several mixed currents among weed banks, over obstructions, under barbed-wire fences, or through a herd of watering bison. They have steady flows, constant temperatures, optimal pH levels, and abundant insect populations. Our spring creeks come in all kinds and sizes, from the huge Henry's Fork of the Snake to tiny unnamed waters on public lands, to which few pay any heed. Some of the spring creeks are pay-to-fish waters, some are open to the public by permission, some will never be open to fishing by anyone other than the owner and his friends, and some are on public lands and open for all to fish, explore, and enjoy.

To know a spring creek is to invest much time on it. It'll be occasionally moody; you must know its attitudes and adapt to changes in them. It'll try to throw an emergence of insects at you at a different time from season to season. In 1995 the pale morning dun emergence on the Henry's Fork, which usually comes off at 10 A.M., came off during the evening hours.

Examples of spring-creek water are stretches of the Henry's Fork and Firehole Rivers, Nelson's Spring Creek in the Yellowstone Valley, and Iron Spring Creek in Yellowstone Park. Short pieces of heavy-water rivers such as the Madison and Gallatin, along with sections of smooth waters such as Slough Creek and the Lamar, can also be spring-creek water.

On spring creeks the fish will be visible, particularly during insect emergences and egg-laying periods, when trout are actively feeding on the surface. During these times you'll learn the most about the creeks' holding and feeding water. Security areas to which trout move during times of fishing pressure should always be noted when located. The largest trout in the streams will always be near security areas.

Look for trout to hold in areas of weed banks, undercuts, and overhanging weeds and brush. Downed timber, sweepers, and the like all provide good cover and food sources, as do bridges and their abutments. Sometimes trout hold in unexpected areas of spring creeks. I've seen large trout holding and feeding in less than 6 inches of water and several feet from cover. Once, after sneaking into position, I saw the largest trout in the pool on my side of the river on the inside of the pool in skinny water with no cover and little current to bring him food. He greedily snapped up every natural that came his way and even moved more than a foot for a fly. In the prime water I also saw several smaller fish grabbing any natural coming their way. Perhaps the larger fish had been hooked before during insect activity so that now—when the other fish began feeding—he moved out of his prime-water hold to escape any perceived pressure. When you're reading spring-creek waters, then, be patient and prepared for the unexpected. Spend much of your time observing, sneaking, and learning each creek, and you will be rewarded by successfully challenging the most sophisticated trout.

SMALL MOUNTAIN FREESTONE STREAMS

When we want to watch a wild native cutthroat trout come up and take a big, bright, bushy dry fly, Jackie and I slip into hip boots, cram our lunch, rain gear, and bug dope into a pack, and head out to explore one or more of the dozens of freestoners in Yellowstone country.

Many mountain streams have all the water types we've already discussed and should be read accordingly. From heavy canyon flows to smooth gentle meanders interrupted by beaver dams forming ponds and sloughs, mountain freestone streams can present puzzles most anglers will seldom have the opportunity to solve. Few are willing to hike—often through bear country—to sample these miniature rivers. That's what mountain streams are—miniature rivers—and they should be read and fished as such.

Usually freestone streams read like an open book. The trout are holding where they are supposed to. In the heavy canyon flows, look for them in the pockets and pools at the bottom of riffles and runs. There are plenty of overhangs, undercut banks, and sweepers to provide ideal holding and feeding water. Rock piles and natural wing dams abound, formed during March when spring remains little more than an insinuation and ice floes work like bulldozers. The fish will be in seams and foam lanes, just as they are in the larger rivers. There will usually be plenty of overhangs, meanders, and smooth glides along the courses of mountain streams. And I know of several spring-creek stretches on mountain streams.

There are few surprises on these waters, yet far too few anglers experience the magic that mountain freestone streams can offer. Most are on the more popular waters that get the most press. But who would not want to find a little jewel of a stream no one fishes—one tucked into the hills and loaded with big trout in its beaver-dammed or meadow stretches? Of course, it might take an hour to hike to it. And thank goodness for all our grizzly bears and their recovery during the past few years: They tend to keep the crowds away. (Most locals now pack pepper spray when hiking into backcountry mountain streams.)

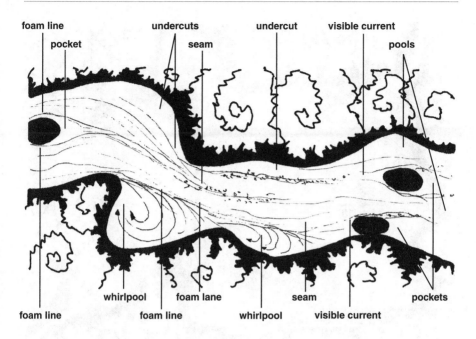

foam line   undercuts   undercut   visible current

pocket   seam   pools

whirlpool   foam lane   seam   pockets

foam line   foam line   whirlpool   visible current

FIGURE 10 – A SMALL FREESTONE STREAM

Examples of Yellowstone-country mountain freestone streams include the Gardner River, the West Fork of the Madison River, the upper Gallatin River, Nez Perce and Tower Creeks, the Little Firehole River, and Middle Creek. But the list of lovely freestoners could go on and on.

LAKES, PONDS, AND SLOUGHS

I don't bet on card games or purchase lottery tickets. But I'll bet anyone that fly fishing Yellowstone country's lakes, ponds, and sloughs will give you the opportunity to take larger wild trout on flies on public water than you'd find anywhere else in the country.

For the dry-fly angler, reading lakes, ponds, and sloughs is best accomplished by becoming familiar with the insect emergences and terrestrial activity that may bring trout to the surface. (I'll discuss these insects in the next chapter.) You should also seek advice from local fly shops and guides, then go out and observe the waters.

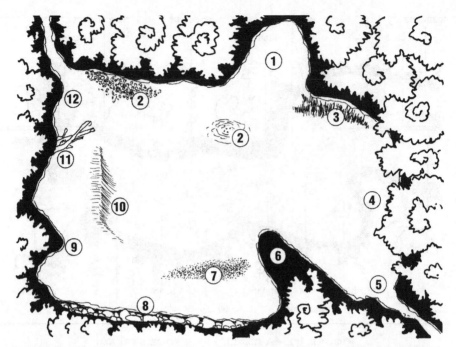

1, cove; 2, weed bank; 3, weed wall; 4, overhanging trees; 5, outlet flow; 6, peninsula; 7, sandbar; 8, bank; 9, point; 10, drop-off; 11, downfall timber; 12, entering spring.

FIGURE 11 – A TYPICAL LAKE

Riseforms will show the way to dry-fly action. Big lakes with no rising trout present flat, seemingly barren water to the dry-fly angler; but if you're on this same water during a hatch, it will suddenly come alive with rising trout.

Wet-fly specialists also have their work cut out for them. Again, it's best to ask the advice of locals, then head out to the lake to observe other anglers fishing.

While learning a lake be alert for coves, drop-offs, shallow gravel bars or sandbars, points, peninsulas, streams and springs entering the lake, and outlet flows. Be on the lookout for sagebrush banks, which provide good late-season grasshopper fishing. Overhanging trees and downed timber can provide fine security areas and harbor food sources. Weed banks and weed walls are tremendously important, as is noting the direction of the prevailing wind and what time it usually comes up. I have heard too many horror stories from anglers who crossed a lake in their float tubes only to be caught in the daily afternoon winds, unable to paddle back across to meet the frenzied spouses who'd dropped them off earlier in the day.

Yellowstone country has hundreds of lakes, almost all of which are underfished. Some are what we refer to as high-country lakes. These beautiful bodies of water are not for everyone, because they often require a hike of several miles. But the fish are almost too easy to bring to a fly. Everyone should enjoy a high-country lake at least once in his fly-fishing life. Nowhere will the scenery be finer, the fish as plentiful or colorful, the air as naturally scented by sub-alpine fir and Engleman spruce. It will be so quiet, and you will be alone.

Examples of our fine lakes include Cliff, Earthquake, Hebgen, Henry's, Trout, Wade, and Yellowstone Lakes. High-country lakes include Grebe, McBride, Rat, Sportsman, and Sheep Lakes.

Ponds and sloughs are much more intimate than lakes, and thus much easier to get to know. Keep in mind, however, that the fish there will be that much tougher to fool.

While not noted for eastern brook trout fishing, our area has some fine ponds that hold brookies the size of those caught in Labrador. We also have ponds and sloughs that contain good populations of brown, rainbow, and cutthroat trout. A few of our ponds are noted for the "tortuga"-sized trout they hold. You will not find any of these places listed here, because they cannot take much fishing pressure. But be aware that there are many such ponds and sloughs in Yellowstone country and around the West. Exploring waters off the beaten path will lead you to several of these areas.

To know a pond or slough you must look for weed beds and walls, points of land extending into the water, overhanging brush and weeds, springs or other sources of water entering and exiting, sagebrush banks (which can provide late-season grasshopper, cricket, and other terrestrial fishing), and any noticeable currents from source tributaries. Trout will hold and often cruise in and out of all these areas. Because most fish seek cover to be safe from predators, the largest will always be near the best cover.

Trout in lakes are almost always on the move, searching for food and swimming with a feeling for the security of the water's depth. Trout in ponds and sloughs, however, are often stationary, facing into the current caused by springs or the dammed stream that forms the pond. Walk the banks slowly, peering over the over-hanging grasses or through streamside cover, to find the trout. Often you'll be able to see the fish in their holding water. Learn where the weed beds are and how the fish use them, if the pond is indeed shallow enough to allow you to view their movements. And be on the water at different times of day in order to learn when and where the trout move, their holding water, their feeding lanes, and their security areas. By successfully reading and learning ponds and sloughs you will be ready to experience some of the finest fishing in the West. You may also find yourself fishing waters that hold some of the largest wild trout in the country.

CHAPTER 4

Skills and Guidelines for Western Fly Fishing

M ost anglers, novice and experienced alike, believe that the most important ingredient in successful angling is the right fly pattern. Yet proper presentation and technique are always more important than fly pattern in providing consistent results on all western water types. As a fly-shop owner, outfitter, lecturer, and fly fisher who spends a lot of time on the water I get the chance to discuss fly selection with many different anglers and to observe their actions on stream. I hear their conversations in the shop, on the water, and at clinics across the country. Too many put their faith in realistic fly patterns. While some would agree that proper presentation is the foundation for all effective fly-fishing strategy, few anglers actually practice its basics.

Too many anglers also rely solely on being able to cast long lines to rising trout. On a favorite spring creek I once watched as the late Ed Zern of *Field & Stream* magazine crept along at a snail's pace, not wading but using streamside vegetation as cover, to get within 20 feet of rising trout in thin water. He then used a short, soft, pinpoint slack-line cast to prevent drag, and took several of the lovely risers. That same day I watched another angler, a man who advocates powerful, fast graphite rods, bang out casts of over 60 and 70 feet. It was indeed fun watching him rip out the long casts. But it was also awful to see the numbers of fish he put down that day by false-casting a brightly colored line over them, dragging his fly through their feeding lanes, and hauling his line off the water, spooking every trout for two pools ahead. This well-known angler did not take one trout all day—but, boy, could he crank out the long casts.

Effective presentation on our waters means knowing your cast, knowing when to wade or not wade, and presenting your fly on as short a cast as possible. Use pinpoint accuracy on a slack line to avoid drag when fishing a dry fly and for most nymphing. Anglers know that their greatest dilemma in dry-fly and nymph fishing on rivers and streams is achieving a drag-free float. On our lakes, ponds, and sloughs, on the other hand, longer casts are often required; I'll take up these special situations later in this chapter.

To begin, though, I'll discuss the guidelines for fishing all western water types. These guidelines apply to all water types but those for which exceptions are noted under specific fishing strategies in the next chapter. They are:

- If you want to fish insect activity such as caddis or mayfly emergences, be on the water when you expect them.
- Check the water, wind, and predicted weather conditions.
- On arrival, take a minute to observe the water and to sample insect activity with a seine. Check streamside vegetation for adult caddis, mayflies, and terrestrials. If you don't find any and you decide to search the water with a fly, pick a pattern that imitates an insect that trout will recognize as something they're used to feeding on.
- If other anglers are present, watch them to determine what direction they're heading in, to avoid crowding, and whether or not they're having success.

- Wade as little as possible and keep a low profile, never silhouetting yourself against the skyline. Wading spooks smaller fish upstream and spoils your opportunities. It also might kill stream insects and destroy trout habitat. It's harmful—if not fatal—to the spawning nests of trout.
- Get as close to rising fish as possible. If you're searching the water during nonhatch periods, get close to holding water before casting.
- Always use a short, soft, accurate slack-line cast. It'll eliminate drag, keep false casting to a minimum, and put your fly on the water in front of the trout. (At the end of this section I will explain how to make this cast.)
- If more than one trout is rising, pick one and cast to it. Never flock-shoot.
- Learn to recognize riseforms. At the end of this chapter I'll tell you how to recognize riseforms to mayflies, caddisflies, stoneflies, midges, damselflies, and terrestrials.
- During heavy rises when the light is fading and visibility is getting tough, always use a short, slack, fixed-length cast. Adjust your position in relation to the trout so that you always know where your fly is.
- Wear earth-toned clothing to prevent sharp, unnatural contrasts with streamside vegetation.

DRIFT-BOAT FISHING ON WESTERN RIVERS

Generally, the foregoing guidelines apply to fishing from a drift boat. If you're being guided, your guide is a professional who knows drift-boat fishing. Listen to him and follow his advice. Typically, you'll be making short, accurate casts to the bank. Most guides will position the boat so that you are within 30 feet of the bank and your target. Since the boat is traveling at the same speed as your fly, you'll have long, drag-free drifts without any need to recast or mend. Many guides will also get out and hold the boat, or anchor it, so that you can fish to rising trout from a stationary craft. When this happens, allow the guide time to get you into a position to cast before you do so. One complaint guides frequently have is about anglers who cast before the boat is in position and thus put the fish down.

Be courteous to wading fishermen. If you're rowing, always give wading anglers plenty of room. Drift by as far from them as possible without bumping your oars or the boat on the river bottom.

FISHING STILLWATER FROM A BOAT OR FLOAT TUBE

Get close to rising trout before casting, and avoid false-casting. When you're moving, make as small a wake as possible, so that you don't put rising trout down. When you're tubing and wearing fins always *back* into the water from the shore—or you'll fall flat on your face. Do not kick your fins when rising fish are approaching. This will spook them. Remember that the rising trout are moving. They must be led, as if you're shooting flying ducks. If they're rising every 6 feet, your fly must arrive at the 6-foot mark or they'll certainly miss it. Finally, if there are weed banks, use them to conceal yourself and your movements. Weeds can dampen the wake of a tube or boat and conceal moving swim fins from trout. Weed banks are also good places to stop and wait for trout to cruise by within casting range, rather than chasing moving fish all over the lake. And weed banks can act as an anchor: If the wind comes up, put your fins into the weeds and they will prevent you from drifting off.

MAKING THE SHORT, PINPOINT-ACCURATE, SLACK-LINE CAST

The primary reason for using this cast is to prevent drag. I have two favorite methods of accomplishing this cast:

First Method

1. Choose your target and carry extra slack line in your line hand. The amount of extra line determines the amount of slack you will be able to put into your presentation. This will come with experience.

2. Guesstimate the spot where you want your fly to land, accounting for current speed and drag.

3. Now, on your forward stroke, aim for your spot. Near the end of your forward stroke check (stop) the rod tip and, at the same time, release the extra slack line from your line hand. This allows your fly to reach your target with enough slack line to delay drag.

Second Method

Steps 1 and 2 are the same as the first method.

3. Aim for your spot. This time, however, follow through on your forward stroke, allowing the fly to shoot beyond your target. When the line straightens, check your rod tip, your line hand, or both. This will cause your line to recoil, creating slack in a series of S-curves. To do this successfully you'll need to develop intuition and feel. With experience it will become second nature.

RECOGNIZING RISEFORMS ON WESTERN WATERS

Remember, while it's important to consider riseforms when you're determining what the trout may be taking, it's never wise to make a judgment based solely on them.

MAYFLY NYMPHS AND EMERGERS

If you see mayfly duns on the water and fish rising everywhere, watch as the naturals float over rising trout. If they let the duns pass, they are most likely rising to nymphs or emergers. If you can see trout tails, it's likely nymphs are being taken just under the surface.

If duns are being taken as they drift over trout, then the fish are obviously taking duns. Or if you see noses, heads, and backs breaking the surface, these risers are taking duns.

If you see a casual, unhurried rise and hear a soft kissing sound made by a trout as he takes an insect, and a slow-spreading rise ring results, these trout are taking mayfly spinners in the surface film.

CADDISFLIES

These three clues indicate caddis emergences and must always be remembered:

1. Trout are leaping out of the water.
2. There are no insects on the water.
3. Most of the rises in faster currents are bulging and splashy. In slower, moderate water look for quiet dimples, porpoising rolls, and tails barely breaking the surface.

STONEFLIES

There is little doubt when trout are taking adult salmonflies. You will see big trout slashing and grabbing adults in swirling rises, or even hurling themselves into overhanging willows to knock adults off limbs. During the emergence of smaller stonefly species, fish may take adults in splashy, aggressive rises.

MIDGES

Midges emerge year-round. On lakes, ponds, and sloughs midges should top your list of insects that rising trout may be taking. On streams from late fall to spring, midges may be the only aquatic insect emerging.

There is nothing unique about a trout's riseform to midges. The strongest clue to an emergence is adult midges skittering on the surface or clustered along the shoreline where trout are rising.

DAMSELFLIES

Rises to nymphs will be quick, darting, knifelike moves to naturals swimming near the surface, migrating to shore to emerge.

Trout rising to adults will launch themselves out of the water after these fluttering flies.

TERRESTRIALS

Riseforms made by trout feeding on grasshoppers, crickets, bees, and flying ants will usually be aggressive, splashy, and noisy. Rises to ants and beetles are subtle, slow, and deliberate.

FISHING MAYFLIES, CADDISFLIES, STONEFLIES, MIDGES, DAMSELFLIES, AND TERRESTRIALS

MAYFLIES

You should first learn which stage of this insect the trout are feeding on. Then get as close to the feeding trout as possible.

Count the trout's rise rhythm. If he's rising every six seconds, put your fly in front of his nose in six seconds.

CADDISFLIES

Since caddis emerge best in the late evening and into darkness, getting as close to the fish as possible allows you to keep track of your cast and fly as the light fades.

Several caddis species offer good fishing opportunities when females lay their eggs. Look for caddis bouncing and flitting on the surface. Also look for spent caddis on the surface of the water, boulders, grassy overhangs, sweepers, and, often, your waders. Female caddis use all of the foregoing to access the water for egg laying.

Even though female caddis move a lot during egg laying, you'll have much more success using a dead-drift presentation. The same holds true for fishing caddis larva, pupa, and spent patterns. A dead drift nearly always fools larger trout.

STONEFLIES

When you're working salmonfly nymphs, fish upstream, dead drift, using a short, heavy leader and tippet. A 6-foot leader with a

0X or 1X tippet is best. Your fly must bounce on the bottom, where the fish expect to see it.

One key to an effective and successful adult salmonfly presentation is flexibility. If dead-drifting an adult imitation doesn't produce, try giving some movement to your fly. Or sink it, or trim the wing and hackle for a slimmer profile. Try every method you know until you start catching fish.

MIDGES

Midges emerge year-round, so you need to be prepared to fish them at all times.

Fish feeding on midges usually hold just below the surface film and are extremely sensitive to wading waves and debris. Midging fish spooked by bad presentations will take a longer time to resume feeding than will fish feeding on mayflies or caddis. This is mostly because they hold so shallow in the water column.

Always present a short, soft slack-line cast to prevent drag whether you're casting to trout working midge pupae, adults, or mating clumps.

DAMSELFLIES

These insects thrive in nearly all stillwaters in Yellowstone country. The thin-bodied nymphs are ineffective swimmers and become extremely vulnerable during their migrations to shore for emergence. They always swim perpendicular to the shoreline, and the fish are accustomed to seeing them move in this direction— hence, it's important to present and retrieve your fly at the same depth and direction that the naturals are traveling.

Adult damselflies are only available to the trout during mating time or windy weather. If you see fish leaping out of the water to chase adult damselflies, this is your clue to try an imitation.

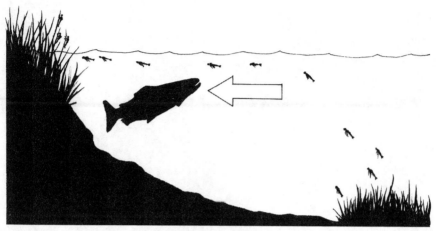

**FIGURE 12 – DAMSELFLY LARVAE MIGRATING
TO SHORE FOR EMERGENCE**

TERRESTRIALS

You can expect to take trout on terrestrials all year long.

While an accurate short slack-line cast is usually best, be flexible in your methods of fishing terrestrials. Try twitching a grasshopper or cricket or moving a beetle slowly if a dead drift fails. The presentation that works today may not work tomorrow.

Since most terrestrial activity doesn't involve concentrations of insects (as do emergences of mayflies and caddis), you're usually prospecting for fish in all the likely holding water. You'll cover more water when fishing terrestrials.

CHAPTER 5

Strategies for
Fishing Western Waters

PRESENTATION AND COVERING
HEAVY WATER

If your schedule allows, you should be on the water when insect activity occurs. Trout are most active during these periods. If you want to fish caddis emergences you won't want to arrive on stream at noon, because most caddis activity occurs during the late-evening hours. Here is where checking with local fly shops, reading, and planning for success are so important.

Heavy, noisy western water can look intimidating to many anglers and downright unfishable to some. In most water types, but especially heavy water, I wade as little as possible. It amazes me to watch anglers literally running into the Madison River with their arms flailing to keep their balance. The pirouetting piscator does little but spook many trout—and usually earn himself a dunking.

Let's look at a typical day of western fishing. You arrive at the stream and find no one parked at the spot you've chosen to fish. Don't string your rod there in the parking area; instead, pick a spot of favorable-looking holding water and sit on the bank to ready your equipment. This way you can watch the water for insect activity and working trout, and check wind conditions. Examine streamside vegetation, too, for any caddis, mayflies, stoneflies, or terrestrials such as beetles, ants, or grasshoppers. With your seine, sample the current's drift and bottom structure for any nymphs; for nymphal or pupal shucks that indicate an emergence of a particular insect; and for mayfly spinners, spent caddis, ants, beetles, midge pupae, or other clues. If other anglers are present, observe them to see if they are having success. To avoid crowding, though, you should also note in which direction they are fishing.

Now decide how you'll begin your fishing day. If you note an emergence of mayflies, caddis, or stoneflies, you'll want to match it and fish accordingly. If no fish are working and you know that, for instance, pale morning dun mayflies have been coming off around noon, you might want to begin prospecting holding water and feeding lanes with a weighted PMD Nymph.

I always cover heavy water with upstream short-line casts of 30 feet or less. Not a fan of strike indicators, I concentrate on the tip of my line to locate my drifting nymph. With only a bit of practice, you'll be amazed at how this allows you to clearly see things under water. Often I can see a trout inspecting or even taking my nymph in the foam lanes or seams. Soon you'll be picking out trout in the heaviest of currents, which will add another dimension to your enjoyment of fly fishing.

If no emergence is expected and I want to nymph-fish, I'll present a nymph that imitates insects commonly found in heavy waters. Usually a stonefly or caddis larva is my choice. I wouldn't use a scud, for instance, because scuds don't inhabit this type of water in the numbers that would make it a strong choice.

If I decide to fish a dry fly when no surface activity is apparent and I find no insects in my examination of streamside vegetation, I pick a fly that imitates an insect the trout recognize. In Yellowstone country that might be a lime-bellied tiger beetle, a red box elder beetle, or a *Hydropsyche* caddis—rather than a cicada or *Hexagenia* mayfly that they've never seen and might not recognize as food.

I walk the banks, wading only when I can't cover a hold or explore a seam or visible current edge from shore. I fish every holding area and pocket slowly, to avoid disturbing the water. It used to be common for western anglers to cover water much faster and less thoroughly than their eastern counterparts. Western anglers were noted for presenting their flies to every likely hold, but not persistently. That's not the case any longer. Given the increased fishing pressure here, you should spend more time trying to fool individual risers, rather than looking for a willing trout at the next pocket. An exception to this might be in cases of expected insect emergences, particularly a mayfly hatch. Due to the microdistribution and extreme localization of some of our hatches, you should explore more water when you expect a hatch. While searching for rising trout and emergences, you should never wade. Walk well away from the banks and observe from there to avoid disturbing the water.

If you wish to fish streamers you should also approach and cover heavy water initially from the downstream short-line-cast position. The primary baitfish available to trout is the sculpin, which is not a strong swimmer. When dislodged from the bottom he will put his large pectoral fins up and turn slightly, which causes him to fall back toward the bottom, much like a fighter plane turning to dive. The most effective method for covering the water here is an upstream dead drift, with the streamer fished nymphlike. You can expect to see and feel the take as you present your imitation on a short, tight line.

I know many anglers who present streamers by approaching from upstream and casting down and slightly across, working their flies against the banks with tight lines. The fly bounces off the bank or lands within a few inches of it. The anglers strip in quickly for a foot or two, then move downstream for another presentation. This is fast fishing and it does take many fine trout. These fishermen also present mice patterns using the same technique—slamming the artificial into the bank and moving it quickly away from the bank. The problem I have with this technique is that when a natural mouse falls into the water it always paddles quickly back to shore. For the best results, then, fish upstream on a short cast and hop the mouse back toward shore.

COVERING HEAVY WATER DURING INSECT ACTIVITY

Most anglers are surprised to learn that there are only four mayfly species, seven caddis, three or four stonefly, a couple of midge, and several terrestrial that offer consistent dry-fly fishing in the heavy waters of Yellowstone country. I'll discuss these insects and corresponding fly patterns in much greater detail later in this book. For now I'll focus on how you should cover the water during their time on the heavy water.

The mayflies on this water type provide some of the finest dry-fly angling of the season. It surprises many local anglers how few visiting fly fishers recognize this, and how many fewer still fish the mayfly emergences and spinner falls successfully. Most visitors to heavy waters believe that the stonefly is king, with perhaps some summer evening fishing with caddis patterns and grasshoppers to finish off the season. Few recognize the importance of tiny *Baetis* mayflies or even the smaller midges—but the trout of the Madison and Yellowstone Rivers feed on these for several months of the year.

Mayflies

When you're fishing mayfly emergences on heavy waters, your first step is to learn which stage of the emergence the fish are taking. Then position yourself about 15 feet directly below working

---

INSECTS

Mayflies: *Baetis, Rhithrogena*, pale morning duns, flavs.
Caddis: *Brachycentrus, Hydropsyche, Glossosoma, Oecetis, Lepidostoma, Arctopsyche, Rhyacophila*.
Stoneflies: salmonflies, golden stoneflies, little yellow stoneflies.
Midges
Terrestrials: ants, beetles, crickets, grasshoppers.

trout. You want to pinpoint your casts, because the fish work in extremely narrow feeding lanes and will never move for a fly, natural or artificial. Also, since the wind always blows on these waters during mayfly emergences, it's best to get as close to the working fish as possible to minimize the wind's effects on your casting.

On rough water trout always appear to be rising to duns on the surface. Cover these risers and observe them closely. Often the fish will let duns pass as they continue to roll in their holding water, seams, and pockets. In this case switch to an emerger, knocked-down dun, or floating nymph pattern drifted in the film at the same level that the fish are working. I like to use a short, set-length cast—never more than 15 feet. This allows me to pick up and recast after the fly has traveled just enough beyond the fish that I can do so without spooking him and can get back out to him without false casting or stripping in slack. I try to count the trout's rise rhythm and anticipate his next rise. Sometimes, if you time everything just right, it seems like you're actually force feeding the riser when he takes your fly.

Fish feeding on spinners are always much more casual in their rises, and they usually work the thin water, shallow seams, margins, quiet pockets, and moderate flows near the shoreline. Rises to mayfly spinners are merely sips.

Although you may frequently observe spinners in their mating flights over the water, it's usually much more productive to fish emergences on these waters. Always be prepared to fish a spinner fall when fish are working this stage of mayfly activity. Remember, gentle, unhurried rises in the moderate-to-slow flows along the edges and margins of heavy, rough waters mean that the trout might be working a spinner fall. This is especially true during calm, warm evenings and mornings.

Caddisflies

Caddisflies are the insects anglers understand the least—and yet they're arguably the most important from a fly-fishing point of view, especially on our heavy western waters.

When a visiting angler first looks down on the Madison River as it gorges its way through the earthquake slide area, he is usually intimidated by its turbulence. The river rips and tears at gnarled snags of timber still standing in its currents. It continually rechannels itself through the 80 million tons of rock and rubble dumped into its path by the earthquake of 1959. The angler's attention often focuses on the heavy flows crashing around huge boulders and the standing waves of white water.

At the shop, when we talk to the uninitiated about the Madison River below Earthquake Lake, we tell them to disregard the middle of the river. Concentrate on the slower pockets, margins, and seams along the edges, and fish the river as you would a small trout stream. If you're here during caddis season, I encourage you to be at the river in the evening, when caddis activity will be strongest. During the late-evening hours the winds lull, ospreys head to their nests to preen their young for the night, casual anglers leave the river for dinner, and the trout begin to rise to caddis emergences.

The best way to approach fish feeding on caddis in heavy water is to make your presentations upstream. This approach usually keeps you from casting across mixed currents; it's also possible to get much closer to working fish by approaching them from downstream.

Some argue that a down-and-across-stream swing is best for caddis pupae. No doubt this method works, but I think the larger trout prefer a dead-drifted pupa. Also, you will certainly break off fewer fish by using the straight-upstream method. Across-and-downstream drifts are made on a tight line in heavy currents, using fine tippets—which often break when a trout takes your offering.

Remember, too, that during caddis times, good fishing opportunities exist when the females lay their eggs.

If you fish a larva imitation, always weight your fly and/or leader. The pattern must be fished on the bottom. Never use a sinking line; such a line does not allow a natural drift.

One method of caddis presentation in heavy waters that has gained much local popularity is using a two- or three-fly cast. Veteran anglers such as John Basmajian and Red Lange have used this method successfully over the past several seasons. If you have a hard time keeping track of a pupa or emerger pattern in the film, you can tie on a higher-floating adult or cripple pattern that imitates the caddis. To the bend of this fly's hook, clinch-knot a section of tippet approximately 12 to 18 inches long. Then tie the low-floating surface-film pattern to the end of this tippet. The higher-floating fly is obviously the indicator, although trout will often prefer it to the pupa.

One important final note regarding caddisflies on heavy waters: Caddis emergences are much more reliable than those of salmonflies. They are responsible for far more larger trout, and they consistently provide the angler with several weeks of solid dry- and wet-fly fishing year in and year out. If you plan to fish our waters anytime during the caddis season—which can run from mid-April through October—study caddisflies and learn effective caddisfly-fishing strategies. The importance of these insects to the trout— and the angler—on most of our moving waters cannot be overstated.

Salmonflies

No other insect creates as much excitement among anglers year after year as the salmonfly. During the annual salmonfly hatch, fishing access sites along the rivers look like flea market parking lots. Motels and campgrounds are jam packed, and guides have been booked solid for weeks. Anglers from across the globe assemble daily to follow and fish "the hatch."

Most years they are disappointed. Rain or snow, runoff, and sporadic concentrations of the insects all produce frustrating angling. This never seems to dampen anglers' expectations. Hitting the hatch once in several seasons makes it worth all their effort, time, and money.

You can use several strategies to fish the emergence of this enormous insect. The most effective is to nymph ahead of the hatch, because the larger trout follow the migration of the salmonfly nymphs to the shoreline several days before their emergence. Not only is this the most effective strategy during this period, but it may also be the only method possible. Sometimes the water is so colored by spring runoff that nymphing with big salmonfly imitations may provide you with your only fly-fishing opportunity.

You should fish upstream, dead drift, using a short, heavy leader and tippet. Avoid wading, which will accomplish nothing except to spook the fish that have assembled close to the banks to take advantage of the naturals migrating to the shoreline in preparation for their emergence. Flies and leaders must be weighted enough that the pattern bounces downstream hitting the bottom, where trout are used to seeing the naturals. Often I "walk" my nymph pattern back to me by giving it a very short upstream cast of 10 to 15 feet, throwing slack at the same time, to allow the fly to sink to the bottom. Once it's stopped on the bottom or is slowly drifting back to me I pick up rod, line, and leader from the water and raise the fly just enough to cause it to bounce-walk back downstream to me. The imitation must bounce on the bottom, ticking, lifting, and skipping in a natural way where the trout expect to see it.

First locate holding water near the banks. Keep in mind that every big fish is near the banks right now. Then get ready for a heavy cast.

Casting a heavily weighted fly and leader requires some doing. Always use a floating line and leader of 6 to 7 feet, tapered down to 10- to 12-pound test. Avoid sinking lines, which will tangle around everything in the stream. Start by paying out 10 feet of line and your leader into the downstream current, allowing it to uncurl and straighten below you. The current will provide the tension needed to bring your cast off the water and upstream. Now lift your rod to the 11- or 12-o'clock position. The fly should be skipping on the downstream surface. You should have a good grip on your rod handle, similar to the one you'd use to hold a hammer. Then hammer the rod handle as though you were striking a nail with a hammer,

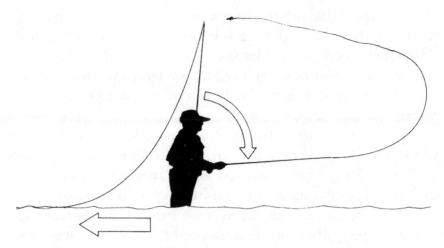

FIGURE 13 – CASTING A HEAVILY WEIGHTED FLY AND LEADER

(HAMMER METHOD)

from the 11- or 12-o'clock position forward to 2 or 3 o'clock, and the fly will whiz by the back of your head and straight upstream in a wide loop. With a bit of practice you'll be doing fine.

The best dry-fly angling with salmonflies occurs when the female salmonflies return to the river for egg laying, usually between noon and four o'clock, depending on weather, which will ideally be bright, windy, and warm. Locating the area on the river where the females are swarming is of utmost importance. Here, the fish will feed on the dry imitations of the salmonfly. If you get above the hatch the fish will not yet have begun to recognize the adults; below the hatch the fish are usually full and no longer looking for naturals.

For the salmonfly emergence, a float trip is recommended. It will allow you to cover long stretches of water and usually enable you to find the egg-laying females.

Trout are often suspicious of adult salmonflies. Maybe it's their sheer size, or their movements when they scuttle about the shorelines. You can expect many refusals of your imitation as fish bump, follow, slap, and splash at your offering.

When you find fish working adult salmonflies, you'll have little doubt that they're taking the naturals. You'll see big trout slashing and grabbing adults with big, swirling rises. Trout will hurl themselves into the overhanging streamside willows in apparent attempts to knock the big adults off the branches and grab them.

Your position when fishing dry salmonflies from a drift boat will almost always be from the side, at 12 o'clock. Short-line casts are best—15 to 20 feet—and you should keep your fly as close to the bank as possible unless you're fishing to a working trout.

If you're wading, approach from straight downstream and search by using a short-line upstream cast to the bank or near holding water. If a working trout refuses your imitation, rest him for a minute, then go right back with a cast, twitching your fly as it gets near his hold. Often it seems like the trout waits for the fly to move. I have pitched many naturals into the stream to watch how fish behave and rise to them. Sometimes they'll take an unmoving natural as it floats by, but on as many occasions I have noted a trout following the natural, bumping it with his nose or drowning it to get the natural to move before taking. Often, skittering or twitching your fly is an effective technique.

If you get no response to your salmonfly patterns even though there are flies in the willows and on the water, try a caddis pattern. Over the past 20 years trout have come to pay less attention to the often-inconsistent salmonfly emergences, and more and more to the predictable caddisfly hatches.

Other Stoneflies

There are other stonefly species that provide dry-fly fishing for anglers visiting the West during the season. The golden and the little yellow stoneflies, for instance, often provide better fly-fishing opportunities than the salmonfly does. Both species are on the heavy waters longer, creating more opportunities for the trout and angler. Also, during their emergences—usually well after runoff—water conditions are more favorable for fly fishing.

Golden stoneflies can be found on rivers such as the Madison, Yellowstone, and Gallatin for a full two months. During periods lacking any mayfly or caddis activity, searching the water with a dry fly imitating this important stonefly can often bring good results. Big trout tend to recognize these insects even when no adults are on the water and will often come a long way to intercept an imitation.

The strategies used to fly fish the golden stonefly are the same as used for the salmonfly.

Blind fishing imitations of little yellow stoneflies during the summer months can often be productive. While the trout never seem to selectively or steadily rise to the naturals, an imitation fished in likely holds will yield some fine fish. Trout may mistake the imitations for caddis, which are usually present when little yellow stones are around.

Midges

When fly fishermen think of midges, heavy water seldom comes to mind. But midges provide year-round fishing opportunities, since they emerge nearly every day of the year. Midges are an important food source, yet they're overlooked by anglers concentrating on stonefly, caddis, and mayfly activity. During the summer months, when these larger insects are emerging, midges are usually not nearly as important as they become from November through April. It's then when midges may be the *only* aquatic insects providing activity on the surface.

It was December 24, a blustery day in West Yellowstone with blowing snow and a stiff southwesterly wind. But it was thirty degrees and the first time we had seen the plus side of zero in a week. Quite often when it's windy and snowy in town, it's clear and calm in the Madison Valley. Since the cold had kept us prisoners of the fly-tying bench for so long, we decided to pack some lunches, throw our insulated waders and fishing gear into the back of the pickup, and head downstream.

At Raynold's Pass we could see Garnett feeding his cattle, using his horse-drawn team to plow through the thigh-deep snow clogging his long driveway and access to his pastured stock. No wheeled vehicle was going to make it through that packed snow. Here in the valley the sun was blinding. There was no wind, and the hoarfrost was just burning off the barbed-wire fences and streamside grass. We finished our hot chocolate in the comfort of the truck and decided to take lunch early, 10 A.M. By the time we finished, it was above freezing. I kept my pac boots on and slogged through a foot of snow to the river's edge.

Midges were already emerging along the shoreline. Clusters of mating midges the size of quarters were rolling downstream in the foam lanes and through the pockets and seams. I saw one clump the size of a baseball rolling through holding water behind a big boulder. Just then, a nice brown nosed into the clump and broke it into smaller clusters. He followed the little clumps downstream, racing to grab each one before it broke over the lip and into the next pool.

We tied on #14 Griffith's Gnats and had a grand afternoon. It lasted until 2 P.M., when the sun's rays lost their punch. Our guides began to ice up and the midge activity stopped for another day.

Midge activity seems to be very localized; extreme microdistribution is the rule. You may walk considerable distances without observing a single adult. Then again, slicks behind boulders and foam lanes where visible currents collect into foam lines, slowing after they pass around islands and downfall, provide optimal conditions for midges to cluster and fish to work them. Water no more than a foot deep and moderate-to-slow flows are the best areas to check for fish working midges. The trout will be in the thinnest water, searching for these insects. They'll also be extremely hard to approach. Often you may get only one float over them. If any drag is detectable or a refusal occurs, the trout may be down for the day. These fish are used to the security of depth, cover, and currents. When you are venturing into thin water to take advantage of midge activity they can at times become almost impossible to approach and take.

Terrestrials

Ants, beetles, crickets, grasshoppers, leafhoppers, and other terrestrials constitute a valuable food source for trout in western waters. For years it was thought that our terrestrial period lasted from August 1 through the end of September. Now we know that this season can last as long as these little armored insects are not covered by snows or freezing temperatures for several days.

Fish the edges and overhanging vegetation, where trout expect to see terrestrials. The pockets, seams, foam lanes, and transition waters all produce.

There's one important exception, however: So much bank walking occurs during terrestrial time, and all summer before the terrestrial period, that trout may head to rougher, more secure water during late summer. I've had fine angling when presenting my hopper or cricket imitations in the heaviest of currents. Water that seldom produces before late summer now seems to come alive as big fish slash and hit huge #2 to #6 cricket and hopper imitations in the deeper, turbulent water. You may have to throw longer casts, pitching in a loop of slack to allow the fly to drift as long as possible before the heavier currents drag it. Fish the white water and heaviest currents, prospecting around boulder and obstructions.

Sometimes terrestrial activity does come through, with concentrations of insects inducing tremendous rises of fish. Flying ants, cricket migrations, swarming bees, beetle flights, and strong afternoon winds can all result in terrestrial insects on the water and fine rises of trout. Once you've determined which terrestrial the trout are rising to, tie one on and present it on a short, slack line to defeat the effects of the afternoon winds. If a drag-free drift is not helping your hopper or cricket to produce, try twitching your fly.

COVERING SMOOTH WATER

Mormon crickets, as they are called, seem bigger than life to anglers first viewing them. The females are almost 3 inches long and chocolate brown to black in color. When migrating they are often seen on roadways, and motorists sometimes swerve to avoid what they believe to be sparrows or small mammals. These gargantuan insects can be found in the beautiful Lamar Valley—home to the river of the same name along with a prized trout stream, Slough Creek. These two streams are classic smooth waters with glides and pools separated by short riffles. Both are wonderful meadow streams with plenty of meanders to cover and lovely wild trout. Most anglers think of terrestrial fishing when considering smooth water. While hoppers, ants, and beetles do provide fine dry-fly fishing, you can also expect mayflies, caddis, stoneflies, and other aquatic insects to bring awesome rises of big trout during their emergences and egg-laying times.

These waters always appear inviting, easy to fish, and full of trout at every bend. Their gentle meadow characters bely their often-fickle natures. They offer difficulties with effective presentation and, at times, even with locating trout.

On smooth water you'll want to spend more time observing and searching for trout than prospecting or fishing blind. If nothing indicates that an emergence is forthcoming I fish a beetle or ant, which I know the fish recognize as food. I patrol the shoreline slowly, looking for a fish to show in a surface rise or subsurface movement, flashing as he takes a nymph. I don't cast on the smooth water unless I observe a trout. If I see one holding but not rising, I give him a dry fly first. I cast the beetle or ant straight upstream or slightly up and across, seldom more than 30 feet. On such water he will most likely come up and take my offering on my first or second cast. Many times he will inspect the first cast and then move back to his hold. Don't be too quick to pull your fly off the water in this case. I've had many fish turn back toward their holding areas—only to race back to take the fly. If you have pulled your fly off the water the trout may, upon searching for it, spot you and spook. Or if he can't find the fly, he often becomes suspicious and won't look at your next presentation. If he doesn't return for the beetle, give it to him again and he'll take it. I'll often spend considerable time sneaking into position for such a presentation rather than risk throwing a long cast and putting the fish on the alert or spooking him altogether.

If you see a nymphing fish, try to determine what type of nymph or pupa he is working. On all smooth-water rivers I've seen trout chasing *Baetis* mayfly nymphs in the shallows and near the banks prior to their emergence. On many occasions I've also seen trout gently sipping midge pupae in the same water type. If you know stream insects, feeding behavior, and rise types, you don't have to spend as much time searching for clues and devising appropriate strategies for fly fishing's various situations.

If you spot a nymphing trout, get into position for the shortest slack-line cast you can make without spooking him. Here you want to deliver an upstream-and-slightly-across or straight-upstream presentation. Put your fly at the depth at which the trout is taking naturals. Just prior to emerging, some mayfly nymphs become extremely active, and trout may chase them into very shallow water. Watch the trout's movement to your imitation. If he takes you can usually see his white mouth open and close, or he may tail up or even chase the nymph, depending on the insect he is feeding on. Sometimes you must get above the nymphing trout and cast a down-and-across presentation to mimic the nymphs rising to the surface to emerge. Other times, in the deadwater near shore where trout cruise to look for migrating nymphs, I have had success presenting a nymph and allowing it to sink to the bottom. Leave it there until a patrolling trout cruises by, then gently pick it up and move it as if it was swimming off. The fish may give chase.

Smooth water can be fished productively with streamers cast straight upstream or upstream and across. Here you want to sneak along the bank and explore the undercuts or any areas offering cover in the form of sweepers and rocks in the main flow. Cast a short, tight line and hang on for the take. Once you make the presentation, retrieve your fly just a few feet—until you are well past the undercut or obstruction—then recast. Many anglers tend to fish out each cast right to their feet, which means they're spending too much time in unproductive water.

One problem you can expect from this water type is fish migration during the season. An area that produces one day may be void of fish the next. Sometimes a tremendous emergence of insects brings no rises in an area that was boiling the week before. Prepare for this by being willing to walk the banks, concentrating and looking for fish.

COVERING SMOOTH WATER DURING INSECT ACTIVITY

Fourteen mayflies, eleven caddis, three stoneflies, and a couple of midges and terrestrials are responsible for the majority of dry-fly fishing in smooth water. I will discuss their emergence periods in greater detail in the chapters dealing specifically with each later in this book.

Smooth water is, again, often considered strictly terrestrial water, though mayfly and caddis angling can be superb. All our smooth waters have some stonefly-water sections, too, so at times we do see stonefly activity on water where not all anglers expect to do so.

Mayflies

My close fishing companion Fred Harrison accompanied my wife, Jackie, and me to Slough Creek last summer. We arrived early, knowing that the gray drake spinners would be on the water by 10 A.M. It was our first trip to the Slough for the year and we were

---

INSECTS

Mayflies: *Baetis*; *Rhithrogena*; pale morning duns; green, gray, and brown drakes; flavs; *Callibaetis*; tricos; pink ladies; *Attenella margarita*; *Serretella tibialis*; mahogany duns; *Heptagenia*.

Caddisflies: *Brachycentrus, Hydropsyche, Helicopsyche, Glossosoma, Oecetis, Cheumatopsyche, Lepidostoma, Hesperophylax, Rhyacophila, Micrasema, Mystacides*.

Stoneflies: salmonflies, golden stones, little yellow stoneflies.

Terrestrials: ants, beetles, crickets, grasshoppers.

excited. I had fashioned a new spinner pattern the night before and was anxious to present it to the big rainbows, cutthroats, and their hybrids on the smooth water. The first fish took in a classic smooth-water cutthroat rise—slow and deliberate. I responded by pulling the trigger too quickly. I barely felt the trout as I yanked the fly from his mouth. We were all guilty of setting the hook too quickly on several occasions that morning, but we managed to finally settle down and have a fine day. Here's an important smooth-water lesson, then: When a cutthroat trout takes your dry fly, allow him to turn away and start down before you set the hook.

On smooth, even stretches of the Lamar, Slough, and Yellowstone during mayfly emergences, larger trout prefer nymphs, emergers, and crippled duns. When you're fishing emergences or spinner falls of mayflies, it's best to approach the rising trout from the side and slightly up or downstream. The trout do not allow as close an approach as they do in heavy water. Also, myriad currents make drag a constant consideration. Watch carefully as your fly approaches a trout. He may rise to it then turn back if he detects drag. Rest him a minute and cast from another position, or throw more slack into your cast for a drag-free drift.

It's common for several trout to be working in one small area, particularly during a heavy emergence of mayflies. Single out one riser and keep the fly in front of him by presenting accurate casts that land softly 2 feet above him. Should he not take, pick the fly off the water a foot or two below his lie. Count his rising rhythm and put the fly precisely on target at the right moment. If you get the fly back to him quickly, chances are he will take.

There is one mayfly emergence every September on the Yellowstone River, and it gives anglers fits. The fly is often referred to as a #18 blue-winged olive, an *Attenella margarita* mayfly, and here is its story.

On many crisp September mornings at the Buffalo Ford stretch of the Yellowstone River, the surface is covered with #18 olive-bodied mayfly duns. A few cutthroats seem to work the duns, yet most anglers, after flailing the water for several minutes, leave the river frustrated. No matter how many times they present with perfect drag-free floats, they cannot buy even an inspection of their dry flies. What is happening here is worth remembering during those mayfly emergences when trout simply will not take a dun. In such a situation the rises you see are fish taking nymphs at the surface. But watch closely during this emergence, and you'll note that the trout not only take nymphs at the surface but also take several nymphs underneath for each one they take on top. What at first glance appears to be a few fish working on the surface is really many fish feeding at a depth that allows no visible riseform. Always keep in mind that even when you see adults on the surface while trout are rising, it's no guarantee that the fish are feeding on them.

In this case, because the fish are feeding on subsurface nymphs and moving around so much as they do so, it's important to fish only to visible trout. On such waters the cutthroats will take a nymph or two; then move several feet upstream, to the side, or down; take another nymph or two; then move again. Blind casting is not effective. You must get into position to see both the fish and your nymph.

The smooth, slick water of the Yellowstone near Buffalo Ford provides ideal conditions for fishing to visible trout working mayfly nymphs. You'll want to pay close attention to light conditions and use them to your advantage when you observe the fish and their movements. Sometimes you'll find yourself presenting your nymph upstream one minute, downstream the next.

Always use an unweighted nymph, which allows you to fish it at the required depth. You may watch as a fish takes a nymph off the surface, then moves several feet and takes another natural or two a couple of feet below. If he is taking nymphs in the surface film, present your fly close to him so that it will not drift below him. If he is working deeper, present your imitation upstream at a distance that will allow it to sink to his depth. The ultimate challenge here is correctly anticipating his movements, getting the fly in front of him at the right depth, and detecting his take of your nymph by sight—because you will never feel it. Anticipate where your fly is likely to be. Any movement toward it by the fish might mean he has it. Watch for him to tip up, tip down, or move sideways. You might note the white of his inner mouth. Gently strike, and often he is yours. And all of this occurs on a 6X tippet with a drag-free presentation. You silently applaud your success, for here you are your own gallery.

Caddisflies

On smooth water, presentation is always critical. Bad presentations mean spooked trout. Whether you're fishing emergent caddis pupa or adult patterns, you should either approach from downstream and present your fly on a slight upstream-and-across angle or approach from upstream, casting across and slightly downstream. The latter approach must be made slowly, to prevent a wading wave from traveling downstream and warning trout of your presence. Either way, it's always best to keep your leaders from floating over your target.

Caddis emergences can be so heavy at times that it seems impossible for your fly to compete with the naturals. Short presentations made quickly and accurately keep your fly in front of rising fish, though, and increase the chances of trout taking your offering. Another effective method is to present your caddis emerger or crippled adult fly across and downstream—but just as it approaches the rising trout, jerk it with a short tug of 2 to 6 inches. This causes the fly to be pulled under, then pop up again in front of the rising fish.

I have fished maddening emergences of *Hydropsyche* caddis on the Yellowstone River. These emergences can last for several hours, their intensity increasing as the evening light fades to darkness. Rising cutthroats are everywhere on the smooth water, porpoising, rolling, dimpling, and tailing after the emerging caddis. The presentations that I've mentioned in this section have always proved to be best in this situation—a major cause of frustration for fly fishers.

Several caddis species offer exciting egg-laying and spent-caddis fishing on this water type. Learn to recognize egg-laying activity and spent-caddis rises. If you're expecting an egg-laying caddis flight and see bouncing or spent caddis on the surface, be prepared to present your fly and cover the water effectively for this activity.

Stoneflies

Generally, anglers do not equate smooth water with stonefly activity, since smooth water is not prime habitat for stoneflies. Exceptions are the canyon and heavy-water sections separating smooth-water areas on rivers such as the upper Yellowstone, the Lamar, and Slough Creek.

On the Yellowstone near Sulphur Cauldron and Buffalo Ford, where there is plenty of suitable habitat for stoneflies, big golden stones can be found fluttering about for almost two months. The salmonfly is also present on the same water, but usually for only a week or two. During July and August a golden stone adult will always raise a cutthroat in the riffles.

Several effective strategies can be used to fish both of these stonefly emergences. Often, water conditions are high and off color during the earlier salmonfly hatch. If so, it's best to nymph-fish the edges and near the banks, because trout are looking for the huge nymphs migrating toward the shoreline to emerge.

Dry-fly fishing is best on bright, sunny, warm, and windy days, which are the rule from mid-July into August in Yellowstone country. Look for trout to be working egg-laying females returning to the water to release their egg masses. On smooth waters it's not nearly as important to locate swarming females as it is on heavy waters. Where short stretches of stonefly habitat are present on smooth waters you can usually count on fish to look for naturals.

Refusals are common when you're fishing big stonefly imitations. Sometimes it's better to use an undersized pattern than one exactly the size of a natural. Twitching your dry fly often brings a take, too, because it seems that the trout are waiting for the fly to move. I've also had fine success using a sunken imitation. Cut the wing and hackle off and pull the fly under water near a fish taking naturals.

Sometimes one fish will be taken on a dead-drifted dry fly, but the next two won't take a dry; they want it sunk. The next trout wants it twitched on his nose before he'll take. As with all stonefly activity, be flexible with your methods.

Midges

During the summer so many other insects emerge on smooth waters that anglers fail to consider midges when they encounter rising trout. But there are occasions when you'll find trout taking midge pupae and crippled adults even though mayfly spinners and spent or egg-laying caddis are present.

Last summer I met an old man who lived in a camper full of cats. He'd just pulled into the overlook parking area across the creek from me. I could hear the howling of coyote pups playing around the century-old Sheepeater Indian tepee rings up on the bench to the north of his tiny camper.

He was lonely. He told me of having fished this water with his wife since the 1940s. Now she was gone. He said he'd wanted to fish it tonight, like before, but once he got to the parking lot he didn't feel like it. We bantered back and forth across Slough Creek for some time. He had been a fireman, I a cop. He went to college on the West Coast, I in the Midwest. He had tied flies for his own use—I had too—and for hundreds of other people. He saw the fish working below his parking spot. I saw them, too. He told me they were on gnats. I told him they were rising to mayfly spinners. I noted a few spinners in the air and even a few on the water. The big risers were really upsetting me. I couldn't fool one. He must have felt my frustration at not fooling even one trout after hundreds of perfect presentations with my pale morning dun spinner.

He threw me an empty tin of chewing tobacco. The can buzzed past my head and made me duck. I hadn't seen it coming, and he apologized. He told me to retrieve the tin and remove the two flies inside it, which would take the trout I'd been unsuccessfully working over for almost an hour now. He said they were "cream gnats"—

what the fish were feeding on. I took the two flies from the tin and pitched his can back to him.

In the wink of an eye he was gone. I wish he had stayed. I only hope he reads this and writes me a letter so we can arrange a meeting and I can thank him.

I bit my squeeze flashlight, turning away from the stream so the beam wouldn't hit the water. I knotted on one of the old man's cream gnats and caught one big fish, then another. Then, like a rookie, I let my backcast drop and lost my fly to a weed behind me. I turned on my light again, this time directing its beam at the water's edge, and there they were—the cream midges I now call gnats.

Midges hatch in the surface film and are very susceptible to "structural" problems during their emergence, so fish usually key in on pupae and crippled adults caught in their shucks and trapped in the surface film. Rises to these naturals are slow and deliberate; the trout take them with confidence, recognizing that they cannot escape the surface.

Presentation during midging activity on smooth waters is best accomplished by approaching the rising fish as closely as possible from downstream, or wading carefully into position from above and slightly across.

TERRESTRIALS IN SMOOTH WATER

Many anglers visiting Yellowstone country during the summer season come to fish the fine terrestrial activity on the smooth waters of the Lamar River and Slough Creek. You should indeed plan to be on the water during the prime time for terrestrial activity. Sunny, warm, windy days are always best for hoppers, crickets, and mating swarms of ants. Both beetles and ants prefer warm, bright conditions, although I have had fine success using them on all but the rainiest days.

Terrestrial time might be the only occasion when prospecting smooth water produces well. I've seen a cricket imitation presented at random in the middle of the Lamar while the angler quickly walked up the bank. The results were impressive. Trout came from considerable distances to take the #2 Slough Creek Cricket, as it's named.

I much prefer stalking the banks, searching for cruising or holding trout as they lie in wait to take an ant, beetle, hopper, or cricket. A favorite method here is to patrol the high banks and bluffs of the Lamar between its junction with lovely little Soda Butte Creek and the canyon water downstream. Every few yards creep up to the sharp banks that overlook the river and lie at the edges, watching the river below. You'll be amazed how many fish inhabit knee-deep smooth water, as well as the runs and riffles that separate the smooth stretches. Pay particular attention to the sunlight; it can help you see into the water and detect the cutthroats, which seem to take on a golden magenta glow when the sun strikes their sides and backs.

It's great sport to fish with a partner, taking turns spotting and casting to these visible trout. Once you find a fish, your companion stays topside to keep the trout in view, while you sneak back from the edge and circle downstream. Trout searching for terrestrials often patrol considerable distances, so it's handy to have someone keeping an eye on your fish so you don't waste time casting to where he *was*. If you're alone try to approach from downstream, not wading, and staying low to the water. Offer no silhouette to the trout, because this will always spook him. He'll think you're a predator.

Try a swimming-to-shore hopper or cricket presentation by throwing a slack-line cast in which you deliver a short section of tippet past the fly. You can do this by checking your forward cast in midair above its target and feeding a foot or two of slack into it just before it hits the water. The extra tippet will land beyond the fly. And if you pull the line in short, rapid tugs of 1 to 2 inches, the fly will move toward that short section of tippet. It's best to deliver this cast so the fly travels toward the shoreline, the way a natural would. This is how trout expect to see a natural swimming back to shore after falling or flying onto the water.

Since most terrestrial activity does not involve heavy concentrations of insects, you must cover more water searching for cruising fish or casting to the overhangs, undercuts, and riffle water separating the smooth-water sections of this fine water type. Keep in mind that trout often cruise considerable distances in search of terrestrials. Fish are likely to be in water where you would not normally expect to find them during caddis or mayfly activity. And cover your backside, too; I've had fish sneak up from behind on several occasions.

SPRING CREEKS

Paul Studebaker had just arrived in town and was on his way to the Firehole. It was a snowy late-September afternoon, which he knew was going to be a good one for fishing the *Baetis* mayfly hatch. Paul enjoys using spring-creek strategies on his beloved Firehole River. And after being gone all summer, he was excited to be in Yellow-stone country again and couldn't wait to get on the stream. There was one purchase he had to make, though. He told us he'd been thinking for a while about a lighter graphite rod than the 6-weight he'd been throwing. He said he was treating himself to a new rod, reel, and line. When he left for the river, his new outfit was strung and ready with a Baetis Sparkle Dun.

When Paul drove up to the river where it runs along the Fountain Freight Road, the *Baetis* were already emerging, and trout were rising everywhere. He got out of the truck, grabbed his new rod, and began to fish without even suiting up in his waders and vest. After he took a couple of wild trout, one broke him off. So Paul set his new rod and reel against a rock and returned to his truck to put his waders and vest on. As he was sliding into the waders, he heard a commotion near the river and looked up: A bull elk was examining his new rod. Paul yelled at the elk, which began grinding Paul's $600 investment into the rhyolite lava rock. Paul started toward the 800-pound bull and the animal headed across the river with Paul's new rod and reel lashed to his antlers by the fly line. The last Paul saw of his new equipment it was heading west, toward the Twin Buttes.

The Firehole River in Yellowstone National Park is a limestone spring creek. It's been described as the "strangest trout stream in the world"; it certainly has some of the finest dry-fly stretches of water in the world. You fish next to erupting geysers, bubbling hot springs, and belching mud pots. Here, too, are classic spring-creek puzzles presenting you with the most challenging fly-fishing opportunities you may ever find.

WHEN INSECTS ARE ACTIVE

Spring creeks always fish best when anglers are prepared for predictable insect activity. I would never fish a spring creek without being prepared for its activity.

Always make sure you know the weather forecast for the day. If it's going to be cool and overcast with precipitation, you can look forward to optimal conditions for the heaviest mayfly emergences.

I try to be on the water well before any expected insect emergence. You might find a nice mayfly spinner fall, some egg-laying caddis, or some other activity that makes an early arrival worthwhile. I've often stalked the banks searching for trout, and I have on occasion come upon big nocturnal browns still patrolling for one last spinner, moth, or caddis left over from the night before. When spooked by anglers strolling the bank, or when the bright sun rays hit the water, these fish retreat to an undercut and stay there until dark.

INSECTS

Mayflies: *Baetis*; pale morning duns; green, brown, and gray drakes; flavs; *Callibaetis*; tricos; *Attenella margarita*; mahogany duns.

Caddis: *Brachycentrus*, *Hydropsyche*, *Helicopsyche*, *Glossosoma*, *Oecetis*, *Cheumatopsyche*, *Lepidostoma*, *Rhyacophila*, *Mystacides*.

Stoneflies: salmonflies, golden stoneflies, little yellow stoneflies.

Midges

Damselflies

Terrestrials: ants, beetles, crickets, grasshoppers.

Once on the water, I string my rod and look for risers. I walk a bit more of the bank and check the drift with a pocket seine. Sometimes I come upon clues, such as drifting nymphal or pupal shucks, mayfly spinners, or spent caddis. If I see no rising fish, I continue slowly stalking the bank for cruisers and for fish holding near weed banks or fallen timber, underneath bridges, or along overhangs and undercut banks.

Generally, blind fishing a spring creek when there is no surface activity is unproductive and accomplishes little but spooking trout. There are a few exceptions, though, two of which affect the dry-fly fisher. The first is terrestrial time, when insects such as ants, beetles, and grasshoppers are active—late June through October. The second is when damsel- and dragonflies are on the water. Damsels and dragons can provide superb dry-fly fishing on spring creeks. Emergences are seldom concentrated—except on the Firehole, where fish chase damselflies in the meadow water above the Nez Perce picnic area during late June. This is one of the only times you can expect to observe big trout throwing caution to the wind and actually chasing, slashing, and splashing after naturals and imitations. When this happens I'll cast a damsel imitation on a long leader with a tight-line presentation. I impart a twitch or quick 1- to 2-foot pull to the fly. That fly should always be presented either straight upstream, up and across on the bank to overhanging vegetation, or near obstructions that protrude from or into the water.

On most spring creeks, searching the water with nymphs during slack insect activity is not worth your time. There are exceptions, such as when you're working the riffles on waters such as the Firehole and Henry's Fork. Here you can do well using soft hackles, caddis emergers, and other patterns imitating aquatic insects expected to emerge or always found in the waters in question. An upstream dead drift is the most productive cast for larger trout. On this kind of water, however, such a cast is extremely difficult. You're wading and fishing upstream in varying water depths, which requires changing weights in your flies and on your leaders. Most anglers prefer to work the riffle water of spring creeks across and down, mending here and there to provide a drag-free float yet still keeping control and the feel of the nymph. This type of fishing on spring creeks usually brings smaller trout, but those who do it always explain that they would rather be fishing than stalking and searching. Me, I'd rather hunt for larger trout.

Our spring-creek water varies from tiny creeks to the medium-sized Firehole to the huge Henry's Fork of the Snake, in Idaho. On the smaller creeks I wade only when absolutely necessary. On the Firehole I often have to wade to position myself for a cast, or to cross the stream to reach a riser. On the Henry's Fork I frequently have to follow rising trout as they work upstream or down, picking off naturals while they move.

On waters such as the Firehole, Missouri, and Bighorn Rivers emergences can be so heavy, with so many rising fish competing for food, that it's nearly impossible to put rising trout down for long—even if you wade right through them.

Spring creeks host the largest and most diverse aquatic emergences in Yellowstone country and throughout the West. Look for eleven mayflies and nine caddis, along with the stoneflies, midges, damsels, and a host of terrestrial species to provide fine dry-fly activity all year long.

Mayflies

Most trout working the heavy emergences of mayflies on spring creeks prefer nymphs and emergers or crippled duns. During emergences and spinner falls I always approach rising fish from the downstream side, and I usually cast to them upstream and across.

Many smaller fish compete for naturals. They get locked into their feeding pattern, which allows you to approach within a few feet. Larger trout sometimes exhibit the opposite behavior: One false cast over a big fish or a seemingly perfect float in his feeding lane and he quits rising, or moves several feet before coming up again.

Get as close to the fish as you can without alerting him to your presence. Do not cast to him until he comes up a few more times.

Let him have a confidence rise or two in case he sensed your approach. While you're watching for his rise, closely observe which insect he's taking, and which stage of the emergence he prefers. On spring-creek waters it is simple to observe rises and determine exactly what the fish is taking. I know several experienced anglers who use binoculars for this task. With patience and stealth you'll be amazed how closely you can approach. I also like to look for the trout and see how it holds and moves in the current, which side of the mouth it's taking flies in, how large it is, and what current it's taking naturals in. Spring-creek water that flows over dense weed banks often has a surface pockmarked by tiny whirlpools. To fish this water you need to provide a longer, slacker tippet to minimize drag. I usually change to a two-pull tippet, one Al Ward showed me years ago on a spring creek in the Centennial Valley.

There was a cold wind and an even colder rain that got the pale morning duns emerging on the water just below the sheep pens. Al always fishes on his knees, which makes the water look waist deep when in fact it's only 6 inches. Wading on my knees, I was determined to make it to Al's side, another 10 yards, feeling every stick and pebble on my kneecaps. When I sidled up to him, Al was changing tippets. He said he had to move to the "no-fail two-pull system." He said that the rising fish was taking naturals on the left side of its mouth, away from us, and that he could not get a good drift. Al explained that the floating weed bed between us and the riser was causing a near-side current that was pulling the fly around and away from the fish just as the fly approached its left side. I watched and, sure enough, as a knocked-down dun floated near, the trout tipped up and took it on his left side.

Al stripped off two pulls of tippet with both arms outstretched, a full 12 feet, and knotted it onto his 10-foot leader. With 22 feet of leader and tippet out, he announced that I could get the camera ready for a picture of a leaping rainbow when it took his Pale Morning Sparkle Dun on the first cast. I got ready and Al presented the fly, which drifted on the right side, our side, of the riser. Not even a look. Al said he had screwed up the cast and asked for another try, explaining that he'd meant to present the fly on the other side, the left side, of the trout. On his next attempt the fly landed "perfect," according to Al. I watched as the long tippet began to unfold and the fly drifted naturally, without drag, the 2 feet around the far side of the weed bank and to the left of the trout. The fine rainbow came up and took, and I captured it all on film.

Many trout prefer one side of the mouth when feeding. The next time you take a fish with a hooking scar or damaged mandible, note where the old injury is and the position of your fly. More times than not your pattern will be in the previously injured area, particularly with a larger trout.

Most anglers wade downstream and cast across to surface-feeding trout on larger water such as the Henry's Fork. This is effective, but it does have the drawback of sending a wading wave downstream, along with all of the disturbed debris, which can put trout down. On waters such as the Firehole, however, where elk and buffalo frequently wade, I've plowed right through stretches of feeding trout without putting them down for long.

Observe closely as your pattern approaches a rising trout. You may see him fin up for a look and then turn away. Rest the fish for a minute and allow him a few confidence rises before presenting your pattern again. Be especially careful to avoid drag, which is usually why he failed to take your fly in the first place. Adjust your position or throw more slack into the cast to compensate for crosscurrents or small whirlpools. You must have a drag-free float.

When you're fishing to visible nymphing fish, approach from downstream and across. Always use an unweighted fly so that you can present it at the required depth. You may see a trout take one nymph off the surface, then take his next few a couple of feet below. If he's taking on the surface, present the fly close to him so it won't drift below him. If he's working deeper, give it to him at a distance that will allow it to sink to his feeding depth. Anticipate where your fly is. Any movement toward it might mean your fish has it. Strike very gently.

Caddisflies

Nine out of ten times when trout are rising and no insects are on the water, a caddis emergence is occurring. Remember the guide-lines for recognizing caddis emergences in chapter 4.

When you're faced with many rising trout and you don't know what they're feeding on, use your seine. Spring-creek waters are so rich in insect life that you'll often find several insect types present in good numbers. With rising trout all around, it's difficult to take the time to haul out your seine and discover the clues the stream is offer-ing. Do it anyway. Once you determine which insect the fish are rising to, you can concentrate on your approach and presentation and not worry about whether you have the right fly on.

Approach a rising fish from downstream and present your fly on a short cast, working it upstream and slightly across. This keeps the leader from drifting over and spooking the rising fish. A drag-free float is always necessary, and it's best accomplished with an 18- to 20-foot slack leader and fine tippets of 5X to 6X. You'll be amazed how close you can approach by patiently wading upstream toward the working fish. My casts are usually no longer than 25 feet, and seldom more than 40. Depending on the stream, I spend much more time getting into position than I do casting long lines, which risks putting fish down with a bad presentation caused by drag or by lining risers. I do whatever it takes, sometimes walking the bank or streambed on my knees, using streamside cover such as vegetation, trees, and high banks for camouflage and cover.

Always determine the trout's rising rhythm if he has one. On spring creeks during heavy caddis emergences it's common for a fish to rise every five seconds, or perhaps to every fifth insect that floats through his lane.

On spring-creek waters several caddisfly species offer both egg-laying and spent-caddis fishing opportunities. You should be prepared to work them.

Stoneflies

For the most part spring creeks are not a preferred habitat of large stoneflies, though some canyon stretches are exceptions. Strategies for these waters are the same as for smooth ones.

Several smaller stonefly species are found on certain stretches of Yellowstone country's spring creeks, however, and they provide fly-fishing opportunities in isolated instances. While I have never observed a steady rise to little yellow stoneflies, I have taken many fine fish by both exploring riffle water and covering a lone rise on a spring creek with an imitation of this insect.

Midges

During the summer, when caddis and mayfly emergences are providing the bulk of spring-creek dry-fly fishing, midges don't often come to mind when you spot rising fish. Many times, however, I've arrived at the stream early in the morning, well in advance of any expected mayfly or caddis activity, and encountered emerging midges.

These insects have saved my day on many occasions when the weather forecast called for precipitation yet the sun was shining. On such days mayfly hatches may not materialize strongly enough to get spring-creek trout working the sporadic emergence of duns; but midges might emerge heavily, bringing on wonderful dry-fly fishing. Keep in mind that even when there are mayfly duns or spinners, caddisfly adults, or terrestrials around, you may find occasional trout that are taking only midge pupae and impaired adults.

I designed the Sparkle Midge Emerger, which represents a crippled midge trapped in its shuck, with two uses in mind. The first was fishing Herb Wellington's private spring creek. Here I could observe big brown trout bulging, taking something off the surface while ignoring the first high-floating pale morning duns of the new day. Initially, I thought the trout were rising to the PMD nymphs. Their rises were similar to those of trout taking a nymph that has prepared to split its nymphal shuck and become a dun at the surface. Unlike those I had associated with midging trout, the rises were aggressive. When I finally did take a fish on an emerging dun pattern and prepared to release him, I saw that his mouth was full of midges. He'd been taking emerging midges, all of them trapped in their nymphal shucks. The Sparkle Midge Emerger is designed to float in the surface film and mimic an emerging, crippled midge.

My second intended use for this pattern was those times when midging trout are taking pupae a few inches under the surface. These fish bulge near the surface, or their tails break the surface as they take subsurface midge pupae in waters such as the Firehole near Goose Lake Meadows. The key to this situation is to let the Sparkle Midge Emerger sink. Using zelon, for the trailing nymphal shuck, and a light-wire hook allows the pattern to either sink or float. If you snap it with a quick backcast, the water shakes out of the shuck and the zelon floats the fly in the film. A lazy backcast, which leaves water in the shuck, and a short pull when it hits the water make this fly sink slowly.

Fishing spring creeks effectively during midging activity is best accomplished by approaching the rising fish as closely as possible from downstream, or by carefully wading into position from above and slightly across. If I must wade, I usually try to approach from downstream, which causes less disturbance and wave action.

Terrestrials

I don't know of a single angler who comes to Yellowstone country expressly to fish spring creeks during terrestrial time. This doesn't mean that these waters aren't productive with terrestrials; it's just that anglers are here to fish mayfly and caddis hatches. Many don't even consider how important terrestrials can be.

Several years back I was visiting Bob Auger, the streamkeeper on DePuy's Spring Creek, south of Livingston. We stood on the esplanade above the creek, just across from the streamkeeper's hut. The morning sun was heating up the bank below us. Hoppers started clicking, and we could make out mating swarms of mayflies dancing above the abandoned ranch house, their wings glistening in the sunlight. The surface of the spring creek just below us was receiving the full effect of the July morning sun; it reflected the rays back at us, looking more like liquid silver than a premier spring creek.

At first the rises were sporadic, and Bob and I thought they came from trout taking spinners from the previous day's pale morning dun emergence. Within minutes rises dotted the silver surface everywhere. I tied on a pale morning dun spinner—my first mistake —walked to the creek, and flailed the water for almost half an hour before deciding to practice what I always preach: Seine the water. I found that the stream was covered with flying ants and the fish were rising to them in a big way. Unprepared, I had to walk back to my truck, half a mile or so, to get my terrestrial box. I returned in time to catch a small rainbow and witness the end of flying ant activity.

On spring creeks the preferred strategy is to stalk the banks for cruising or holding trout while they search for ants, beetles, hoppers, and crickets. Flying ants swarm much the way mayfly spinners do and often fall onto the water, thereby creating a "hatch." But most terrestrial activity will be sporadic and you'll have to patrol the banks, searching for trout.

It helps to use the sunlight to your advantage. It can greatly assist you in locating fish below the surface. Always try to position yourself with the sun at your back, and be careful to keep your shadow off the water. This is an optimal angle that reduces glare and improves vision.

An accurate, short, slack-line cast is often the best approach on spring creeks, but don't be afraid to try different tactics. On one spring creek in Yellowstone National Park the brown trout patrol the overhanging vegetation and deep undercuts. They'll take any terrestrial pattern—as long as it's a big beetle slapped down on the water with a *plop*. Herb Wellington taught me this technique several years ago on his water. I had tied him several foam beetles with elk hair legs. When I presented them to Herb, he said, "Not enough bulk to cause a *plop* when they hit the water." Try as I might, to this day I have not proved him wrong. The bulky beetle does bring fish from under the banks, however—sometimes from a considerable distance.

Since most terrestrial fishing doesn't involve an emergence or heavy concentrations of insects, you must fish more water, covering overhangs, undercuts, weed banks, and riffle waters to find cruising fish. An exception is swarming ants or bees, which fall or fly onto the surface of spring creeks and produce fine dry-fly action for those prepared with an imitation. All serious spring-creek anglers carry flying ant, wasp, and bee imitations. Some anglers pack these flies around for years without any occasion to use them. But come upon a flying ant swarm or a mating swarm of bees without them and you'll never want to be unprepared again.

Usually beetles, ants, bees, and wasps should be fished upstream with a short slack-line cast to avoid drag. Keep in mind that trout often cruise considerable distances searching for terrestrials. Fish will often swim up behind you, or they may appear in water where you wouldn't usually find them during mayfly or caddis emergences. Be flexible in your method, approach, and presentation. Sometimes I've had success pulling ants and beetle patterns beneath the surface as they approach a cruising trout. The fly then pops to the surface in front of the fish and he rushes to take it. Other times I have purposely hung a cast with a beetle in an overhanging piece of vegetation. If I then raise the rod or pull slowly on the line, the fly dips to the current and then rises with a yo-yo effect —which can prompt vicious rises from the usually gentle bank sippers.

MOUNTAIN FREESTONE STREAMS

Probably no single kind of stream in Yellowstone country holds more secrets, water types, and insect activities—yet receives less angling attention—than this one. Many little freestone jewels feature heavy water as they roar down their tiny valleys from high above. Some have smooth meadow sections mixing pockets, pools, long glides, and rapids on their way to joining larger rivers. Some look like spring creeks for short sections where they enter beaver ponds or stillwater sloughs. Below the beaver or natural dams they usually gain speed, becoming freestoners again.

I don't want to sound censorious, but too few anglers visiting the West spend time exploring and learning this water type. It's often full of surprises—fine insect activity bringing lovely rises of wild trout with few, if any, other anglers.

ED WOOLSIE, JIM BEAL 1923 is carved into the overhang above the door of a dilapidated log cabin Jackie and I discovered just a few yards off a mountain stream, a small tributary to the Gallatin River. We'd been on this stream several times before but had never walked up a short spring inlet that came in from the north. Here we discovered the old cabin with its wood-burning stove and creaky wooden beds still intact on a level piece of ground above the spring. The spring bubbled out of lava rock, and watercress was thick at the source. We added it to the elk salami sandwiches we had packed for lunch.

Jackie and I come to this mountain stream every July. It is then that a green drake mayfly emerges in the meadow stretches, bringing up fine rainbows, cutthroats, and their hybrids.

When you first see this stream from the highway, it appears too fast and shallow to hold any significant trout. After several years of driving by, though, Jackie and I noticed another local's car parked there. I asked Larry about this stream when I ran into him one day while I walked my police beat. He said that since we'd been in town for a few years he figured we were "local" enough to know that the stream did hold a few nice trout for those willing to walk up a mile or more. On our next day off we were on our way.

Be aware that quite often these busy mountain freestoners have sections of meadow water and, usually, a beaver dam or two along their courses. On such stretches the character of the stream can change from mountain freestone to that of a smooth spring creek or a pond or slough, requiring changes in your strategies and techniques.

On classic freestone water, which has plenty of riffles and runs, pockets and pools, overhangs and sweepers, fish always hold where they are expected. That's where you should search during periods lacking insect emergences and rising trout.

Freestone streams are usually cold, originating high in the mountains. Often these mountain streams are the last to run clear and free of spring snowmelt. Their insect emergences can also be expected later than those on the large flows that warm earlier. Emergences are always unpredictable, however, due to erratic early-spring weather, which often includes tremendous April and May snowfalls. These late snows postpone hatches or force them, in heavy runoff years, to occur during periods of high and turbid water.

Such unpredictability makes it almost impossible to do the kind of planning for freestoners that you can for other water types. You'll want to be prepared for almost anything once the water clears of snowmelt for the season. Because the water temperatures are often so low, insect emergences and dry-fly activity seldom happen before noon and usually cease early in the evening except on the warmest summer days—but note that on local mountain streams last summer, there were only two evenings above sixty degrees!

I take a good selection of high-floating dry patterns for searching freestone waters, along with a selection of small streamers and general nymphs that imitate the caddis, mayflies, and stoneflies I expect to find. I also bring dry imitations of these insects, along with my terrestrial box. A pair of hippers or wading shoes is usually adequate.

It's often best to cover a lot of ground to find the prime pockets, pools, and meadow water present on so many freestoners. Otherwise, much freestone water is barren of all but the smallest trout. If the stream is fast and offers no security or protection from the current, keep going until you find better holding water.

Cast to each good-looking hold, but only once or twice before moving on. Trout will usually respond on your first cast.

Always work upstream. Present a short slack-line cast and dead-drift it whether you're nymphing or using a dry fly. I seldom wade this water unless it is to cross here and there for a better cast when I sneak up on a pool, pocket, or overhang.

Freestone streams can often be fished effectively with streamers worked straight upstream, using either a dead drift or a rapid, jerky retrieve. Try both retrieves to determine which the trout prefer that day. It often changes daily.

FREESTONE MOUNTAIN WATER DURING INSECT ACTIVITY

Because of the varied nature of this water type you should be prepared for any and all insect activity. Trout rising on freestone water will invariably be easier to fool because they haven't experienced much fishing pressure or seen many fly patterns during the season. But be prepared to use spring-creek and stillwater tactics.

Mayflies

I know many of you will raise your eyebrows at this heading. You haven't yet experienced a stretch of smooth meadow or spring-creek water on a freestone stream just as its wild trout are rising to an emergence of mayflies.

Clayton Molinero specializes in such situations. Last August we hiked in to a freestone stream where we fully expected to fish terrestrials all afternoon. As we ate lunch a thunderhead came over the pass, feeding on the afternoon heat and building to tens of thousands of feet in height. Thunder and lightning bombarded the surrounding ridges, forcing us to leave our graphite rods on the bank and head to safety nearby. When the show was over, fish were rising to an incredible emergence of green drake mayflies and we had a field day—until the next batch of thunderheads rolled in an hour later.

But the fact that trout in this water type tend to be a little easier to dupe doesn't mean you can get away with a sloppy presentation or approach. In the smooth stretches, these fish will be as spooky as their cousins downstream. It's common for fish to rise to a mayfly emergence in this water type, using a pool, run, or long slick between meanders for their feeding area. Cover is always nearby, so if they're spooked they'll be down for the rest of the emergence.

You'll usually find several fish rising in a pool or run during an emergence of mayflies. Trout feeding in meadow stretches will often move in their holds and feeding pools, taking advantage of every insect coming through. They don't have the luxury of heavy or long-lasting emergences, as trout on other water types do, so they tend to be a bit greedier. By getting as close to a feeding fish as possible you can see him take your fly—and therefore you can often let a smaller fish spit it out without hooking him and disturbing the entire pool. Many times I've allowed several smaller trout to race in front of a larger fish, take my pattern, and reject it. I then let the fly drift clear of the smaller trout before picking it up and presenting it again, hopefully to the larger rising fish. Once you hook and play a fish in the pool the rest are normally alerted and spooked, and they won't rise again.

I've never seen an emergence on this water during which the fish rose specifically to nymphs. Usually they prefer crippled or fully emerged adults on the surface. Any imitation with a trailing nymphal shuck works well, and it helps to use a fly with a high wing, such as a Sparkle Dun, so that you can keep track of it at all times.

An extremely effective presentation on this water is one English anglers have used for centuries: dapping. Sneak along the bank, keeping a low profile. Look for the outside, deepest part of a meander. Without casting, you can often dap your leader, tippet, and fly on the water in front of rising trout just off the end of your rod. Use streamside vegetation, high banks, and any cover to conceal your approach.

If you're fishing a rise of trout to mayflies, position yourself about 15 feet directly below a working fish. Determine what the trout is rising to and present a pinpoint cast. Freestone fish work in extremely narrow feeding lanes and won't move for naturals or artificials outside them—they probably don't even see such flies.

The only places I've ever seen trout rising to spinners are those where the stream is smooth or spring-creek-like. During calm, warm early evenings or late mornings, the rises will be gentle and unhurried in the meanders and moderate-to-slow water.

FIGURE 14 – DAPPING A FLY

Caddisflies

Caddisflies provide anglers on freestone water with several weeks of solid dry-fly and wet-fly/pupa fishing throughout the season. The importance of caddis can never be overstated. Be prepared to fish their activity on freestoners from the moment the water clears to the steady snows of late fall. I've fished a #14 Rusty Caddis of an unknown species on sections of this water in the fall, and it provided me wonderful dry-fly action.

Caddis emergences on freestone streams usually occur during the late afternoon and seldom last much past darkness—yet they bring on strong rises of trout. Fall emergences can come on during the heat of the morning and into the afternoon, however, depending on the weather.

I prefer using a crippled caddis imitation for emergence, egg-laying, or spent-insect fishing on this water. The X Caddis is easy to see and, with its trailing shuck, imitates an impaired caddis, a stage the trout recognize and are comfortable taking.

Stoneflies

Stoneflies are always present in freestoners, and I'm sure that on some waters of this type salmonflies can be important, too. On the freestone mountain streams I fish, I've never known salmonflies to provide a significant emergence—with the exception of the Gardner River. Still, fishing a salmonfly nymph has been very effective on them. Since it requires the same approach and presentation as that used with the golden stonefly nymph, whose adult is always important on this water type, we will examine both methods here.

Clawing our way down into the canyon last July was much like a mountain goat hunt for Jackie and me. The big salmonfly hatch had ended the week before and been a bust, due to high, muddy, cold water. The Gardner was still running a bit high and off color, but it lacked the mud and cold snowmelt of the previous week. The canyon water ripped around boulders and sloughs, and off layers of the shalelike rock that litters the riverbed in places. The water was a bit intimidating at that time of year, nothing like the easy upstream flows above Sheepeater Cliffs.

But golden stonefly husks were on the rocks, and Jackie and I knew we'd do well that day. Wild rainbows came to almost every cast into a likely looking hold below the big rocks and slides. We were enjoying a break from the difficult spring creeks we'd been fishing recently. It was fun to throw short, hard casts at the rock walls and watch our big imitations being fought over by feisty 10- to 14-inch rainbows. Then a large black bear decided to approach with her two cubs, one chocolate brown, the other so black it looked maroon in the sunlight. When the chocolate cub saw us he stood on his hind legs with his hair on end, frizzing as though he was being shocked. We decided to head up out of the canyon.

If you must wade, approach from downstream and use a short upstream cast to the bank or any likely looking holding water when you're nymphing or searching with a dry imitation. If you're working a rising trout and he refuses, rest him a minute and then cast again, twitching your fly as it nears his hold. Imparting some movement to your fly often brings immediate results. Dead-drifting, twitching, floating, and sinking your dry imitation should all be tried when you encounter uncooperative fish.

If you should come onto an emergence or some egg-laying activity of one of the smaller little yellow stoneflies, fish an imitation in the likely holding and feeding water. While trout seldom seem to selectively or steadily rise to the naturals, an imitation blind fished in the likely spots will yield some fine trout—even when all else fails.

Midges

The general character of freestoners does not provide optimal opportunities for midging—although the spring-creek, smooth-water, and pond/slough sections of freestone mountain waters do. Keep in mind that midges emerge year-round, and fish may feed on them anytime on all water types. Be prepared for this activity.

Terrestrials

If you've never fished a freestone mountain stream, you owe it to yourself to spend a summer day fishing terrestrials on one of these delightful waters. During this all-important time for trout, ants, beetles, grasshoppers, crickets, leafhoppers, and other terrestrials constitute valuable protein-rich food sources. The trout seem to know this and, as the winter season approaches, increase their patrols of this water type.

Almost any terrestrial or high-floating pattern will bring trout up for an inspection. One favorite of local anglers is the H & L Variant, which imitates a butterfly common on western waters during August and September. While the debate goes on as to the effectiveness of butterfly and moth patterns, trout continue to rise to the H & L, and it can always be counted on when you're searching freestone streams.

Fish the edges, overhangs, sweepers, and foam lanes. These are all places where trout expect to see terrestrials that have fallen into the water.

Searching likely looking holding water and feeding lanes with terrestrial patterns is your best bet. Try the seams, pockets, foam lanes, and transition zones with careful, short, drag-free presentations covering all likely looking water. Do not dally, for around the next bend might be a spring-creek or smooth-water section with larger trout rising to terrestrials or late-season caddisflies.

LAKES, PONDS, AND SLOUGHS

I still have the photographs I took of Nick Lyons on the slough he immortalized in a chapter of his lovely book *Confessions of a Fly Fishing Addict*. He was puffing a pipe then, almost 20 years ago. One of the shots was taken just after he landed his first fish. Nick has a look of surprise, his pipe falling from his clenched teeth. I can still hear him sucking on the pipe stem and saying, "My god, Craig, these fish are tortugas!" His quote is penciled into my fishing log still, along with that photo of Nick, the tortuga brown trout, and the beaver dam in the background that formed our beloved "Tortuga Bay."

For years we would tease fellow fishers by asking "Do you know the way to Tortuga Bay?" And then one spring the beavers left, their dam fell into disrepair, the slough filled in with silt, and the tortugas were forced to leave. Such is the cycle of beaver ponds and many sloughs in the West. Other ponds now take Tortuga Bay's place. I'm pleased to report that this year, after 10 seasons without Tortuga Bay, a beaver family has moved in and repaired the dam. The bay has returned, and in a few years I'm sure the tortugas will also.

Most anglers visiting this wonderful country will never fish a slough or beaver pond holding big wild trout. Most will never cast into an alpine lake, or even one of the readily accessible lakes in the valleys. Yet such waters give anglers a better opportunity to take huge wild trout on flies on public property than anywhere else in the country, and perhaps the world. Last year, guide Bill Schiess and his fishermen on Henry's Lake boated more than 60 fish in excess of 30 inches in length during our short summer season. Most of these trout would average 12 pounds or better.

Visiting anglers who want to catch and release a rare wild Montana grayling often ask where to accomplish this. For those willing to stroll into Grebe Lake in Yellowstone National Park, the task is really easy and fun—yet few make the 3-mile hike.

WHEN INSECTS ARE ACTIVE— AND WHEN THEY AREN'T

If you want to fish dry flies, be prepared for mayflies, caddis, midges, damsel- and dragonflies, and terrestrials. If this isn't your game then grab your sinking line and check out points of land, places where tributaries enter the main lake, coves, drop-offs, and weed banks. When the surface is empty of insects you must look to subsurface fishing, or to searching likely looking areas, with terrestrials, damsel- and dragonflies, leeches, scuds, cranefly larvae, mayfly nymphs, mice patterns, and more.

Few anglers try to fish western lakes and ponds with mice patterns. Charlie Brooks talked about it, and only two individuals I know still try them at times, one of whom hangs out at the Grizzly Bar near the West Fork of the Madison River. He heads up to Hebgen Lake several times during the summer to throw mice flies onto the shore, then drag them off into the shallows wherever tributaries such as Cherry and Trapper Creeks enter the lake. He does this after midnight until he gets tired, usually around 3 A.M. I promised him I wouldn't mention his name. He takes his share of browns—never rainbows—up to 9 pounds.

INSECTS

Mayflies: *Callibaetis, Tricorythodes*.
Caddisflies: various members of the family Limnephilidae.
Midges
Damsel- and dragonflies
Terrestrials: ants, beetles, crickets, grasshoppers.

Searching lakes when no surface activity is occurring may seem fruitless, and at first it can certainly be frustrating. After all, there are often thousands of acres of water with little obvious character or definition to show you where the trout might hold, feed, or patrol. It may look like a silver desert when it's calm, or turn into a float tuber's worst nightmare when the afternoon winds come witching.

When you're searching lakes, always seek out weed banks, springs and tributaries, outlets, coves, and other anglers working the water to show you where to begin. I paddle or motor out and pick a fly that I know the trout will recognize as food. A leech is a good pattern to start with, as is a cranefly larva, scud, or damsel- or dragonfly nymph.

At first I use a full-sinking line, one that gets down in a hurry and remains at the level at which I began retrieving my fly. Some lines don't maintain their depth once the retrieve is started. Avoid them. The best lines are the Scientific Anglers Uniform Sink IV full sinker, and the Cortland 444SL Quick Descent full sinker.

I vary my depth and retrieve with each cast, move about, and cover as much water as I can. Always count as your fly line sinks. I let my fly tick the bottom on the first several casts, then fish higher in the water column. By counting each cast down I can determine with each take what level the trout prefer and adjust my subsequent presentations accordingly. I remain alert to other anglers in the area and approach closely without disturbing their water, watching their retrieve, depth, and, hopefully, what fly they're using. A few lake regulars might talk with visitors, but no anglers are as secretive as lake fly fishers.

Cover all likely holding and cruising areas. If you're float tubing, pay close attention to wind conditions so as not to be caught off guard and blown to the other side of the lake.

Use a slight breeze to your advantage if you're tubing or in a boat. Drift along and cast a mayfly nymph, leech, cranefly larva, or tiny scud, trying different retrieves and depths as you move.

On a few occasions searching lakes with dry flies can be productive. Look for sagebrush banks, which might host grasshopper mating activity in the afternoon. Overhanging trees and other wooded areas are often responsible for ant- and beetle-fishing opportunities.

I watched Cam Coffin last September on his favorite lake presenting a parachute hopper against a sagebrush shoreline. Cam could take a fish on every cast. His secret was to cast to the shoreline, twitch his fly once or twice, and then let it sit. Sometimes it would take a minute and other times it would happen immediately, but he would raise a fish on every cast. He'd then rest the water for several minutes and enjoy the scenery before making another presentation.

Searching ponds and sloughs when insect activity is slack is another matter. Because they're smaller and not as deep, sloughs are more intimate and easier to get to know than larger lakes. Remain patient and avoid needless movement. Trout in shallow ponds and sloughs lack the security that deeper water gives to those living in lakes. Thus they're always much tougher to approach and present your fly to.

I enjoy stalking the banks, searching for holding and cruising trout. I look for weed banks; for structure that provides cover, such as fallen trees and brush; and for points of land that jut out into the pond or slough. These are all favorite places for large trout to hold. Beaver lodges, the deep runs that beavers use to enter their bank houses, and the deep water directly in front of beaver dams are always good spots for trout. And where springs enter the main pond, fish congregate for the food and cool water.

Nervous water created by a trout moving and searching for food should always be investigated. Whether you can see the fish or not, cast well in front of his wake. Allow your fly to sink, then twitch or move it slightly on his approach.

On some lakes, ponds, and sloughs there will be current. Holding fish usually face into the slightest of currents. Carefully approach from the downcurrent side and, if possible, right from the dam. Then take a break and scan the deeper water above the dam. I've often seen big trout holding here, apparently resting or even asleep in the security of the depths. Walk with extreme caution. The ground here is usually soft and will telegraph any careless, quick, or heavy movement to these extremely spooky fish.

For example: You note trout holding a few feet above the dam. You decide on a small scud pattern and work out a short-line cast. Your first presentation looks fine in the air—but as soon as it hits the surface the trout bolt for cover. What happened? Sometimes these trout simply cannot be fished to. No presentation can be made without spooking them. These are not rare occurrences, and I wish someone would tell me what to do in them. Still, these are the unsolved puzzles that keep us returning to the water time and again.

At other times, though, the trout spook due to careless presentation. The leader or fly might have slammed down on the surface; a glint off your rod or your movement may have been detected by one of the several sets of eyes below the surface on full-time alert for predators from above. I have had my best success here using a long leader—say, 18 to 20 feet tapered down to 5X or 6X. When the trout takes it is not necessary to strike; just pull your line taut and let the power gum in your leader absorb the shock of his weight and the power of his runs and jumps.

Try presenting a small fly imitating the *Callibaetis* nymphs often found in these waters. Trout recognize these nymphs as food sources and are usually comfortable taking a properly presented fly. I like a #16, unweighted. Using as few false casts as possible, deliver your fly (if you can sneak in close enough) by casting it with the leader only. It should ideally land on or at the shoreline, never less than 4 feet away from your target. Let it sit. If it landed on the shoreline vegetation and your fish is, say, 6 feet away, give it a little pull and let it slide into the water. If it landed in the water, let it sink to the bottom. The trout will often approach it. Do nothing until he is within a foot of your fly, then slowly begin a steady 6-inch strip. *Callibaetis* nymphs can swim rapidly. The trout knows this, and he'll often rush your nymph to take it. Let him. Don't pull the fly away. (Of course, that's always easier said than done when you're watching a tortuga-sized brown on a mission to take your fly!)

Use the sun to your advantage when you're searching and stalking this type of water. I'm always amazed by how well a cruising brown trout stands out in the sunlight. Often you will see his shadow as he moves over weeds or a contrasting bottom. Sometimes you'll see his dark bronze back coming from underneath an overhang or nearby weed bed if he hasn't yet had time to change his colors to match the sunlit bottom.

Stalk patiently, staying well back from the bank. Never blind-cast unless there's wind, chop, rain, or snow to obscure the surface film and prevent trout from seeing your line and fly hitting the surface.

The little pond in the Madison Valley was formed during the gold rush of the late 1800s. A family had moved in and dammed the tiny spring creek that fed and formed the pond. They farmed the water for trout—so the story goes—to sell to the miners. They're long gone, of course, and so are the mines, but the pond still has browns, rainbows, and a few cutthroat trout. Several years ago we took our daughters to this pond to teach them pond fishing. The surface was smooth, and we could see several trout milling about but not feeding. The girls were young then and perfectly content to practice casting on the upper end of the pond. We could watch trout scurry for cover when their casts hit the mirrorlike surface. A short time later the wind came up, producing waves on the pond and causing problems with their casts. Both kids wanted to bail out and head for home. The wind brought on a chill, and their tangled leaders were enough for them to call it quits. We encouraged them to spend a little more time fishing, and we moved down the pond to a spot where the current bit through weed banks and formed deeper channels.

Both girls cast their damsel nymphs into the channels and began immediately to strip their flies back quickly. Both wanted to get "a few more casts" done with quickly so we could be on our way.

But both were hit immediately, and both landed beautiful little browns. Several more casts produced similar results. The wave action was disguising their crude presentations, and the fish were hungry. A short while later we were trying to talk the kids out of their rods so *we* could make "just a cast or two," and the wind chill was suddenly gone.

Mayflies

Joe's barking told me Lin was into another Hebgen Lake gulper. Joe sat in the front seat of the old boy's pickup truck, watching and waiting for another fish to make Lin's reel talk. Every time that reel screeched with another strong run Joe would bail out of the front seat and hit the water swimming, barking all the way out to Lin's float tube. There, the little terrier would perch on the edge of the tube until Lin landed the trout. Then Joe would swim back to shore and get back into the truck, waiting for another chance. Lin is one of the best gulper fishermen I know. This is some of the most challenging and demanding fly fishing there is, and also some of the most rewarding—if you use the right strategies.

The term *gulper* was coined by Bud Lilly many years ago. It refers to trout on Hebgen and other western waters that make a distinct gulping sound as they cruise about, taking dry flies off the surface.

There are three main mayfly species you need to concern yourself with on western lakes, ponds, and sloughs. The largest is the gray drake, the *Siphlonurus occidentalis*, which emerges fully a #12 and comes off Yellowstone Lake in Yellowstone Park. The next mayfly to emerge is the speckled-winged spinner, the *Callibaetis americanus*, #16. It is the most important from a fly-fishing standpoint because it emerges on most lakes, sloughs, and ponds. The smallest mayfly, commonly referred to as a trico—*Tricorythodes minutus*, #18 or #20—is important on Hebgen Lake.

The gray drake is one of the West's largest mayflies, emerging sporadically on Yellowstone Lake in July. While you can't count on this mayfly to bring on a good rise of trout every day during this period, if you do hit a spinner fall in the morning or evening, you'll never forget it.

The nymphs of the gray drake can also be important to lake fly fishers. Gray drake nymphs migrate to the shoreline to emerge, and I've found that stalking the shoreline can be productive. If you watch the margin from the shoreline out several feet, you can often find patrolling cutthroats searching for these nymphs in selected places along Yellowstone Lake. I have had my best angling in areas near the outlet of the lake and down toward Pumice and Gull Points.

If you find a cruising trout, you must present your unweighted nymph well in front of him. Allow it to sink, and as he approaches to within a few feet, begin to retrieve in short, quick strips of 2 to 6 inches. Yellowstone Lake cutthroats are usually very approachable; often I can wade to within a few feet without spooking them. I like to get above where they are cruising and present the fly down and slightly across to them. A bright, sunny day is always best, because it allows you to spot their magenta sides and golden backs from a distance. When a fish takes your nymph you will see his white mouth open, and he may turn. The take of a Yellowstone cutthroat is always slow and deliberate. It is very easy to strike too quickly, even when the fish is taking a quickly retrieved nymph. Give him a slow, careful strike, either with a hand strip or by holding your line tight and raising your rod. This is fine sport, wading and sight fishing, and you will return to try it again and again.

The duns of the gray drake emerge sporadically. They tend to emerge on or near the shoreline and are seldom concentrated. You won't usually find trout rising specifically to duns, although a dun imitation will seldom be refused by a rising trout.

Yellowstone Lake cutthroats prefer spinner falls of gray drakes. They are usually concentrated and come down on the water from 10 A.M. to 1 P.M. If the wind drops and the temperature stays steady, there might be another fine spinner fall from 7 to 10 P.M.

I prefer to fish rising cutthroats working gray drakes on Yellowstone Lake by wading, not tubing. Not that tubing is ineffective; I just find that I can approach and present my fly to more fish quicker by wading. I can also see them better, get into position faster, and stay warmer longer by wading. Tubing in this lake can be uncomfortable, because the water seldom reaches 50 degrees.

Single out one fish and note his direction of travel. Position yourself so that he will pass within casting range. Lead the trout by the same distance he is rising between his insects takes. Usually cutthroats feeding on gray drakes will not exhibit the classic gulping behavior you see among trout rising to *Callibaetis* and trico mayflies. There just aren't enough gray drakes on the lake to cause gulping.

Callibaetis emergences and spinner falls present lake, pond, and slough fly fishers with classic gulping behavior. Several trout will be rising to naturals at the surface, connecting their rises every few feet as they feed on adult mayflies. Here you must single out one fish and determine his direction of travel, making sure he will pass within casting range. Pay close attention to weed walls and the edges of weed banks. An approaching gulper may run into a wall and then change direction, heading back the way he came; or he may travel with the weed wall, always parallel, never penetrating the weeds.

If you're fishing from a float tube or boat, make sure you don't create waves by motoring or kicking into position. Trout meeting this type of wave will always change direction. It's always amazing to see a trout working into a wave created by a boatload of non-fishermen cruising by, because the fish never stops gulping! If it's your wave he will, of course, change direction and head out of casting range. Somehow he knows.

Keep false casting to a minimum. It's important to lead the riser by the same interval as his gulping rises. If he is coming up every 2 feet, lead him by 4 to give your fly time to settle. The distance between gulps is most likely related to the number of the naturals on the water. The more mayflies on the water, the closer together the gulps will be. You must also present your fly on target. A rising fish will not move out of his lane to take your fly, and he will seldom break his rhythm once he locks into coming up at a specific distance.

When you've presented your fly, it's important to allow enough time—keeping in mind the fish's distance—so that you can pull slowly on your line to remove the slack in your tippet and force your fly to come around and face your position. If you fail to do this your fly will drag, even in stillwater. The tippet is trying to straighten out, uncurling in the film, and your fly is dragging slightly on the surface. You can hardly detect the drag, but the trout can, and you'll experience many refusals and false rises unless you pull your tippet straight, making the fly cock true and face you.

Often the spinner falls of the *Callibaetis* will coincide with the emergences. Seldom do trout show a preference when both are present on the water. Present your fly as I've just explained.

Trout working *Callibaetis* nymphs are always a rewarding challenge. Often you will see splashy rises around midmorning, as the trout chase the active nymphs. Last summer Phil Takatsuno, who spends more time fishing lakes during mayfly season than anyone I know, taught me a great lesson. We were checking out weeded areas of Hebgen Lake in preparation for the morning's emergence of *Callibaetis*. Phil gave me his rod, which was loaded with one Callibaetis Sparkle Dun and two nymphs—a three-fly cast. In a section of open water just off several weed banks we noted a few rises, indicating that the fish were chasing the swimming nymphs. Phil positioned his boat in the heavily weeded area and told me to cast my fly into the opening where three trout were nymphing. He said to let it settle and then give one steady 8-inch pull and leave it. I followed his directions and the Sparkle Dun disappeared like a bobber being slowly pulled under the surface. Before I struck, the rainbow felt the steel and took to the air. This happened a few more times that morning before the trout locked onto the duns. Phil explained that trout usually take a nymph with such confidence that they travel several feet before rejecting it. He says they often set the hook themselves: They feel the fly and bolt, causing the line tension to drive the hook home.

Wind and currents in this water type often produce what local anglers refer to as scum lanes and slop troughs, both very important to fishermen.

Scum lanes are areas where the current meets weed banks or other currents and forms lanes that collect insects in great numbers along their edges. I've seen scum lanes on Hebgen Lake over several hundred yards long. On smaller ponds and sloughs these lanes may be only a few yards long. Usually they are narrow—never more than a few yards wide.

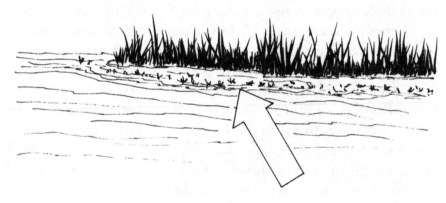

FIGURE 15 – SCUM LANES

Slop troughs are calm sections of water that have not been disturbed by winds in the late morning or early afternoon. These sections are large, often several acres. Several scum lanes might come together with weed banks on a slop trough to present thousands of insects to hundreds of trout collected there. Hundreds of rising trout sound like farm animals feeding at a barnyard trough. Around 2 P.M. the afternoon chop takes over and the water becomes too rough for surface feeding. Scum lanes and slop troughs should always be explored for rising fish and insect activity.

Wind can play a significant role in *Callibaetis* fishing on lakes. Often smaller ponds and sloughs are unaffected. If the wind is blowing before *Callibaetis* activity, regardless of how many duns emerge or spinners fall, trout will seldom rise. If the wind ceases

FIGURE 16 – SLOP TROUGHS

before an emergence, however, you are often in good shape—even if it comes back up slightly. If trout are rising to an emergence before the wind comes up, they will continue to work both it and the subsequent spinner fall, as long as the wind doesn't produce whitecaps on the lake. Actually, a light wind is best. It allows a closer approach, the fish are less wary, and they may even move farther to take an imitation.

Fishing *Tricorythodes* emergences in Yellowstone country is generally limited to Hebgen Lake.

Tricos have a few peculiar emergence and mating characteristics worth studying. The small males emerge at night and seldom offer fishing opportunities until the next morning. Then they return to the water with the larger females that come off in the early-morning hours. Here, during the morning emergences and spinner falls, the fish rise and give anglers wonderful dry-fly action.

The nymphs of tricos are not worth imitating in this water. However, trico dun and spinner activity can bring fine rises of big rainbows and browns that gulp both stages on the Madison Arm of Hebgen Lake.

If you wish to fish tricos, arrive early. These insects may emerge as early as 6 A.M. The lake must be glassy calm. If there's any wave action, trout won't rise to this tiny insect. A float tube or boat is necessary to cover this activity effectively. Also, as with *Callibaetis*, if there are enough duns to get the fish gulping in regular, rhythmic fashion, you can expect good fishing if you follow the techniques outlined for proper presentation on pages 104–5.

One other characteristic of tricos is that they tend to emerge in the middle of the Madison Arm, or of any area that was once a river channel. They'll be well out from shore—unlike *Callibaetis*, which emerge from weed beds and along the shoreline in addition to out in the middle of the lake.

Caddisflies

Not much is known about caddis fishing on lakes, ponds, and sloughs in Yellowstone country. I've had wonderful late-evening action on Hebgen, Earthquake, and Grebe Lakes, along with many smaller ponds and sloughs. Our friend Woody Wimberly, a year-round resident of Yellowstone Park, tells stories of fine caddis activity on Lewis Lake as well.

July and August are the best months to expect caddis activity on this water type. All the activity I have fished has been in the evening. The calm, warm evenings of mid- to late July seem best.

Look for surface activity to start as soon as the sun falls below the tree line. In July this happens late—never before 9 P.M. If trout are working caddis emergences they'll invariably rise aggressively. I've seen fish chasing, slashing, and leaping completely out of the water as they rose to emerging pupae and skittering adults.

On this water type, unlike the others, you will *see* caddis as they emerge. You should use a crippled adult pattern with a trailing shuck, such as an X Caddis, which floats and skitters well. Present the fly in front of a rising fish and strip it into his path. A 6- to 18-inch rapid strip is best. Most often you will have to guess at the direction the trout is traveling, as his rises are seldom linked enough to provide a clue. Try skittering, skipping, or pulling your fly under, and then let it sit for a few seconds before you move it again. Rarely will risers be selective to pattern, and often you're blind fishing, because trout show themselves only occasionally.

Last July Phil, his golden retriever Luke, and I arrived on the Madison Arm of Hebgen Lake around 7:30 P.M. We rigged and headed out onto the lake. Patrolling the south shore, islands, and coves gave us cause for concern. We saw neither caddis nor rising trout even though the wind had dropped and it was warm. Were we too early in the season for this emergence? We had both fished it in the past and our logbooks showed that it was time. But then the sun dipped below Horse Butte, the sky took on the look of a Charley Russell painting as trumpeter swans hailed the evening on their way to their feeding grounds in Yellowstone Park, and the trout came alive to emerging caddis. The fish aggressively ambushed emerging, crippled, and skittering adults. Phil and I flailed the water, Luke barked enthusiastically, and we had a great time landing a few respectable trout before an evening thunderstorm came in at 9 P.M. This activity went on nightly for a full two weeks. We never saw another fly fisherman casting to the rising trout. This can be exciting angling for large fish—and very few anglers have tried it.

Damselflies

The damselfly is an important food source for trout and an important insect for fly fishers. It is found in every pond, slough, and lake in Yellowstone country and the West.

The nymphs I tied were all unweighted and the perfect color to match the naturals I had collected the previous week. The lunches were ready and I checked all our gear for the steep 3-mile walk the next day. (Clearly, I would not have to work out on the NordicTrack the next night.) Big rainbows patrol the edges of this tiny pond, always on the lookout for a damsel nymph or dry. Jim Utterback and I had checked it out a week earlier and the nymphs were ready to emerge anytime. It was mid-July and the adult damsels had always showed then.

When we arrived the little pond was already alive with rising trout. We ran down to the water expecting to see damsel nymphs migrating to shore to emerge. At our first look, though, we saw *Callibaetis* spinners literally blanketing the surface. Without another glance at the water we prepared to present our mayfly spinners to the rising trout. Jim waded in first; he'd not experienced this before, and the sight and sound of big rainbows apparently gulping spinners was more than he could handle just sitting back and watching.

A short while later I was geared up. But Jim had not taken a fish on his *Callibaetis* spinner in the meantime. Something was wrong. Of course, I had to fish a spinner for some time before realizing what it was. What really brought me to my senses was noticing several light olive damsel nymphs crawling up my dark brown Gore-Tex waders to complete their final molt before emerging. The nymphs were so camouflaged in the water that we never saw them swimming by us on their way to shore to emerge. The trout were not rising to *Callibaetis* spinners; they were gorging themselves on migrating damsel nymphs after all. Fortunately, I had tied all those perfectly colored, unweighted damsel nymphs the day before. We trudged to shore and tied some on. I wished I had tied more. We ran out after a few fish and tried weighted versions without nearly the same success.

What happened here is typical of damselfly emergences. Surface-feeding trout will not move even 1 inch down in the water column to intercept a slightly weighted nymph. Also, they will seldom take a nymph presented parallel to the shoreline. The natural nymphs always swim directly in to shore or to whatever structure they choose for emergence. Trout recognize this behavior and seem to key on it. If your presentations don't re-create the exact line and depth of the naturals, they will be ignored.

Damsel nymphs are always more important than adults. They should be fished on a tight line, delivered in front of cruising fish, and retrieved in steady 3- to 6-inch strips. When fishing to visible trout always use a floating line and long leader to avoid lining and spooking the cruising trout.

If you're fishing deep water during damselfly activity, use a full-sinking line and cast it perpendicular to the shoreline. Retrieve with a steady short strip. The trout are accustomed to seeing the naturals swimming toward shore, and any deviation from this migration trail will be ignored.

Some of our lakes and all of our ponds and sloughs offer good adult surface fishing during damsel periods. Trout take adults whenever they can. On ponds and sloughs, I prefer to stalk the banks and search for a visible fish, presenting an adult damsel imitation within a few feet of where it's lying or cruising. If the trout fails to take a dead-drifted fly, give a twitch or 2-inch pull on the next cast and hang on.

For blind fishing on larger waters such as lakes, present the adult fly along overhanging vegetation, weed banks, islands, or any other likely looking holding or security areas. Try twitching, skittering, or pulling the fly under, then allowing it to pop up in front of a cruising trout.

Midges

Midge activity on stillwater produces special problems for anglers. Most fly fishers are not prepared to successfully meet these difficult situations. They simply refuse to fish midge activity—or they fish it unsuccessfully, blaming their poor results on their fly pattern. But if you know midge behavior, where and when to look for them, and proven strategies to fish their activity, you can always expect good results.

Wherever trout are found, so are midges. Lakes, ponds, and sloughs provide ideal habitat for these insects. On such water, midge activity—which stimulates more trout rises than that of any other insect—should always be suspected when you encounter rising trout.

Midges emerge throughout all seasons. Anglers fishing lakes, ponds, and sloughs must always be prepared to meet and fish midge activity.

There is nothing unique about a trout's riseform as he takes midge pupae or adults from the surface film. Often the strongest clue that fish are feeding on this insect is the sight of adult midges skittering along on the surface or clustering along the shoreline while trout are rising. I look forward to fishing midges every chance I get.

The first snow lily has opened in the aspen grove in our back-yard. Its bright yellow face is a sign of spring, even though most shaded areas haven't entirely surrendered their snow yet, and won't for several more days. The aspen buds are still locked up tight, not giving any clue as to when they'll unfold. But the moose are back. Their black winter coats are now a dingy gray, faded by the long, hard winters of Yellowstone country. I check my logbook and find that they have returned here to their calving and summer range in my backyard between May 6 and 12 for the past several years. My log also tells me it's time for early-season midge emergences on Hebgen Lake, because the ice usually comes off the lake around May 10.

Anglers in the West miss exciting dry-fly fishing to big cruis-ing trout if they fail to learn midge fishing on lakes, ponds, and sloughs. Since most activity takes place during calm surface condi-tions, I arrive either early or late in the day. During the spring, just after ice-out, midge activity is strongest during the warmest part of the day, as long as the water is calm. Because our nights are often still cold at this point, late afternoons and evenings are your best bets for finding good midge activity on stillwater.

On lakes such as Hebgen, Earthquake, Cliff, and Wade, I usu-ally arrive around 5 or 6 P.M. Big water means fishing from a float tube or boat. On most smaller ponds and sloughs, though, I prefer to wade or fish from the shore. Before I enter the water I spend much time observing from shore, with binoculars if necessary, to determine where in the lake the fish are rising the most strongly to midges. This can change from day to day, minute to minute.

I gear up, get in my boat, and carefully head out to approach the risers, taking care not to cause waves on my approach. Approaching within casting range, I am ready with my two-fly rig. One is a pupa, the other a crippled midge with a trailing shuck. I can always see the crippled pattern, and it floats in the film where the trout are used to taking pupae and impaired adults.

I never make a presentation to a riser more than 50 feet away. Carrying that much line in the air while keeping track of my flies and the working trout usually results in a bad presentation, a missed rise to my fly, or a blown chance at a closer-rising trout. I know it's easier said than done, but it's always best to be patient. Rather than risk spooking rising trout, hold your fire until a fish gets closer and your presentation can be properly made. Thirty- to 40-foot casts are ideal.

Trout working midges often connect their rises in a rhythm, rising every few feet—a behavior known locally as tracking. These are the fish that will respond best to properly presented flies. They are locked into their feeding rhythm, gulping insects every couple of feet just as they do during the mayfly activity I discussed earlier (see page 102).

I've often seen approaching risers spook at anglers' backcasts, so keep false casting to a minimum. If you're fishing from a boat, keep as low a profile as possible. Standing on a casting platform or seat is fine until fish get within 50 feet. Sometimes they will see your silhouette or movements and quit feeding.

Trout often work in pairs and sometimes in packs of four. They travel along until they locate several midge pupae emerging, or crippled adults caught in their shucks and trapped in the surface film. You may see them wheeling and circling as they rise to the naturals in an area no larger than a kitchen table. If you come upon this situation, so much the better: You are almost certain to get a hit. Competition becomes a factor as fish race to each natural. Properly presented, then, your imitation stands a greater chance of being taken by one of several rising trout. Finding a pack of midging fish is one of the only times flock shooting works. Present your next cast among them as they feed like hungry wolves. Be ready for the strike, which should be gentle to protect 6X tippets.

Seldom is a dead-drifted midge pupa or crippled adult taken. Tom Young, a well-known local fly fisher and an innovative fly tier, taught me a valuable midge-fishing technique many seasons ago. Tom reports having learned it from Dick Walker's fine book *Trout Fishing*. It seems that as midge pupae rest vertically in the surface film prior to emergence, they can "feel" the approach of a trout. When alarmed, they dive for the bottom. By casting in front of a rising trout and drawing the pupa or crippled adult slowly and steadily through his path, you simulate this behavior. This active method of presentation is usually best for taking rising trout on lakes in Yellowstone country. It also works great on ponds and sloughs.

One final note on presenting midge patterns during rises: Try smacking a rising trout on the head with your fly. I've seen times when emergences of these insects were so strong that it seemed trout either didn't see or ignored the fly. So I hit them on the head with a cast as a last-ditch strategy. Sometimes it works well. Try it if all else fails.

During my discussion of covering mayflies in this water I talked about slop troughs and scum lanes (see page 106), and how they concentrate insects during emergences and activity periods. Be alert for the same phenomena during midge activity, because fishing sloughs and ponds during these periods requires similar techniques—with a few differences. On these smaller waters fish rising to midges will travel less, because currents deliver pupae and crippled adults to them. On such waters I therefore patrol the shorelines—not wading—and search for rising fish. And I do whatever it takes to approach rising fish closely here. I often walk on my knees or crawl into position using streamside vegetation and anything else to cover my approach. Trout rising to midge activity on this water are extremely wary.

Depending on the current, or lack of it, I want the fly to land where it will not spook a rising trout yet will be close enough for him to see it. Midges do not fall from above, and trout are not used to seeing them crash down out of the sky. They are used to seeing them suspended or trapped in the film and diving to avoid predators. I like to wait until a trout is rising to a natural to make my cast. Timing and keeping track of the trout's movements and rises are therefore critical. Be patient and wait for a good opportunity. Once a trout starts up to take a natural, present your fly within 2 feet of him. Allow the fly to come to him. Never drag the fly into his lane. A natural would not behave that way; trout recognize this and spook. First try a dead-drift presentation. If the trout fails to notice it, follow with the same cast—except that as the trout approaches give the fly a slow pull, 2 to 4 inches, as if to mimic the natural moving off from a fish's approach. This is real cat-and-mouse fishing and some of the most challenging there is.

There's a tiny slough in Yellowstone Park that we fish once a year. We'll spend an entire afternoon there, usually in late August. Afterward we have dinner at Old Faithful to celebrate our success fishing midges on this water. The most successful day we have ever had there was four trout hooked and two landed. The fish are indeed wary. They're mostly browns, although I once caught a rainbow, and we've taken a few small brook trout. The largest trout I've ever seen in Yellowstone lives there. She's several pounds heavier than my best fish to date, which was a gorgeous male of around 5 pounds. I had her on once. She took one of the small brookies I had hooked on my crippled midge, but I pulled the tiny trout out of her chomping jaws. She raced around the slough, searching for the little guy that had escaped, and I got a good look at her as she stopped a few feet in front of me. Between my thumb and index finger I held a short piece of tippet, my fly, and the little brook trout, still hooked as he tried to revive near the shore. Should I bait fish with him? The huge female was right there in front of me, waiting.

Terrestrials

While not noted for providing steady terrestrial activity, lakes in Yellowstone country often surprise visiting anglers with wonderful action. Still, for the most part this activity should not be expected. With the exception of flying ants, terrestrial fishing is usually sporadic.

Up where the mountains snag the clouds there are many fine high-country lakes. During late summer you can walk the banks, picking off trout as they cruise the shoreline in search of hapless insects that have fallen into the water. If you're willing to invest a bit of time and effort hiking to these lakes, you can experience a type of fly fishing few others have.

On many western lakes grasshoppers provide fun summer dry-fly fishing. I prefer to find a sagebrush slope or hillside, which is usually loaded with hoppers. During the late morning and early afternoon the insects become active, flying and clicking about the sage in an attempt to find a mate. Often the strong afternoon wind gusts knock some of these insects into the water, where it seems that waiting trout can never refuse them. Approach such an area slowly, and watch for any cruising fish. More often than not you will locate fish, and blind casting a hopper imitation can bring good results.

Begin by presenting your fly just off the shore—within a foot of the bank. Try twitching your imitation or presenting it dead drift. Leave the fly on the water for several seconds, keep false casting and continuous presentations to a minimum, and don't let the fly sit on the water too long. After you take a fish, wait several minutes before presenting your fly again. Then, if you do see searching trout, go right back to them with another presentation.

Other terrestrials that can bring rising trout up on lakes are beetles, ants, and flying ants. For searching this water during the summer months a beetle or ant imitation is a fine choice.

I like to stalk the banks to spot cruising or holding fish under trees, along deadfalls and stream vegetation, or near weed banks. If the light is right you can usually see any trout holding in such areas and present your fly to them. If you don't see trout it's more of a chuck-and-chance affair. But if you find the right holding water you can usually bring them to an imitation. Spend time in all the likely looking security and holding areas. Spend more time stalking and searching for visible fish than casting blindly. If you inadvertently spook a fish, make a mental note of where he was and come back after giving him time to settle. Chances are good he will come back to the same spot. By being careful on your next approach you may take him.

Flying ant mating swarms can bring on tremendous rises of trout. Every August, usually around the middle of the month, many of our western waters host tremendous flying ant swarms. Fish relish these insects and rise aggressively to them. What first looks like trout rising with a splash to caddis during the heat of a calm August morning usually turns out to be trout feeding on flying ants. It's quite a sight, and anglers fishing lakes in the West during August should always be prepared for it. During flying ant activity on lakes the rises seldom resemble classic gulping behavior. Instead, the trout feed greedily, moving quickly and taking several flies in quick succession before pausing, maybe to swallow, and then coming up a few feet later for several more gluttonous rises. You must get on such a riser quickly. Put the fly right on his nose, and if he moves put it on him again. The activity seldom lasts long, but if you have the proper fly and can present it quickly enough you will do well. This is one case where rising trout on lakes can be hard to put down. They become so preoccupied with their feeding that you can get away with almost any approach. If the insects are swarming heavily and coming down on the water in large enough numbers to get the fish frenzied, even slapping the fly on their heads or making waves won't put them off the feed.

On ponds and sloughs terrestrials can provide superb dry-fly angling opportunities. I often search the shorelines, weed banks, inlet and outlet areas, and other holding water for cruising or holding fish. A beetle or grasshopper delivered hard off the bank will often bring a vicious rise. If trout seem shy or spooky, an ant delivered lightly on a fine tippet right over their holding spot will almost certainly bring a look. As always on ponds and sloughs, keep out of sight and look for fish. Blind casting usually does little except spook trout in the smaller ponds and sloughs. Work up-current slowly, and spend extra time looking for trout, staying well back from the shoreline to mask yourself and your footfalls. Banks are often honeycombed by beaver, mink, and muskrat tunnels. Any heavy walking sends vibrations through the water, warning fish of your approach.

Here's a final thought: Use competition among cruising trout to your advantage. When two or more fish are cruising the same area, present your fly between them. Usually they will both race to take the fly. May the largest trout win.

PART THREE

The
Flies

CHAPTER   6

Notes on Fly Patterns, Western Hatches, and Other Insects

T here are incredible populations of aquatic and terrestrial insects that provide fly-fishing opportunities in Yellowstone country—and most fishermen pay much of their attention to the fly patterns that imitate these insects. Many anglers collect flies, some frame them and put them in their dens or offices, and many try to tie their own.

G. E. M. Skues was likely the first angling author to discuss the phenomenon of trout feeding on emerging nymphs and mayfly duns not yet clear of their nymphal shucks. Later, in his 1931 book, *The Flyfisher and the Trout's Point of View*, Col. E. W. Harding talked about emerging duns splitting nymphal envelopes. He discussed how important it might be to imitate the nymphal shuck. He believed that an emerging insect moves and shakes its shuck in an attempt to escape, causing the shuck edges to shimmer. Harding is the first author I can find to speak about "sparkle" in connection with mayflies and caddisflies.

For *Caddisflies*, Gary LaFontaine developed a series of emerging caddis imitations that use sparkling pupal shucks effectively.

And in *Fly Fishing Strategies*, Doug Swisher and Carl Richards brought stillborn and nymphal shuck imitations to the fore.

The idea of imitating nymphal-pupal shucks trailing behind newly hatched, crippled mayflies and caddis has thus been around for some 65 years.

Once, on the Henry's Fork during a heavy emergence of pale morning duns, we were reduced to seining and observing insects after large rainbows had refused everything we'd presented that day. We noted many emerging duns trapped in their sparkling nymphal shucks. This simple observation changed our fly tying and has improved our fishing ever since. Some of the patterns John Juracek, Clayton Molinero, and I subsequently developed are detailed in *Fly Patterns of Yellowstone*, Volume 1. The most important mayfly pattern is the Sparkle Dun. Since then we've created other important patterns, such as the X Caddis for crippled caddis, the Zelon Midge, and our "Knocked Down Dun" mayflies.

I have a video of Nick Lyons taken during a pale morning dun emergence on a local spring creek that shows him landing several nice brown trout. (Nick had no idea the camera was running.) We discuss fishing in general, the weather, family, and business. Toward the end of the tape Nick hooks and releases a lovely brown and says, "I never feel confident fishing a mayfly hatch unless I have one of your Sparkle Duns on." The pattern has also proved successful worldwide, as have the X and Irise Caddis and other flies incorporating trailing sparkle shucks.

Any list of fly patterns will reflect the fishing style and preferred water type of the angler who compiles it. Keeping this in mind, I believe that the selection of flies I list with each insect in this chapter reflects the varied waters available to anglers exploring the West.

While there are many other patterns effective for fishing the various hatches and insect activities I've covered, the ones here are local favorites and proven flies. My list should prepare you for an entire year of insect emergences as well as cover all other fly requirements for western angling. Yet it is really quite short, and if you do not fish certain rivers or at certain times of the year it shrinks even further.

Few anglers take the time to really learn our insects, their behavior, when and where they emerge, what imitations of them to present, and how to fish these imitations to be successful in the sport we enjoy. In my experience with thousands of anglers I've found that some don't have the time to learn insects, some don't want to learn insects, and others know little but the difference between a mayfly and a caddis. And while most agree that a knowledge of insects can greatly improve success, I have discovered that very few know where to begin. Let's try to solve that problem here.

In 1992 John Juracek and I wrote *Fishing Yellowstone Hatches*, which described important insect hatches of the area. This guide has been so well received that it's in its third printing. In this chapter I will summarize the sections of *Fishing Yellowstone Hatches* that deal with insect emergences. Because of the incredible wealth of insects thriving in this area, both aquatic and terrestrial, it's possible to find fish feeding on them every day of our season. Let's examine these emergences and get an understanding of how important each is to fly fishing. I'll describe their behavior, how they relate to fishing, when and how each insect emerges, techniques for fishing these insects, and more.

It will be quick and painless. And I think you'll be pleased by how much this knowledge will add to your fly-fishing success and the pleasure you take in this grand sport, and by how easy and uncomplicated it really is.

MAYFLY
EMERGENCES AND ACTIVITY PERIODS

While there are probably more than 100 species of mayflies inhabiting waters in the West, only 15 provide anglers with consistent activity year in and year out. These 15 are responsible for nearly all the mayfly fishing you might encounter in the Yellowstone area during the entire season. If you fish only certain waters or certain times of the year, the number is even smaller.

Though mayflies hatch nearly every month of the year, May to October is when most of these emergences serve as important food sources for trout. Knowing when and where to expect the heaviest mayfly activity is paramount to success on many waters.

The heaviest mayfly emergences take place on cool, overcast days. Rainy or snowy conditions are ideal. Still, while this type of weather produces the heaviest hatches, it's not a requirement for good emergences. Strong hatches can also be counted on during warm, sunny conditions—it's just that the best fishing during mayfly emergences comes in inclement weather. That is when the emergence is usually heaviest; also, the insects ride the water longer and experience more emergence defects during poor weather. Finally, you can usually get much closer to rising trout during bad weather, probably because trout are more comfortable feeding under overcast skies.

Fishing mayfly spinners, on the other hand, requires warm, calm conditions. Strong wind, a cold temperature, or precipitation prevents them from reaching the water to lay their eggs.

THE MAYFLIES

Tiny Blue-Winged Olives—Baetis Species

The first mayflies of the season to emerge are commonly referred to as tiny blue-winged olives. Two species of this mayfly emerge during the early season and are important to anglers. The *Baetis tricaudatus* is the first to make its debut each spring, around May 1. The second species is the *Baetis punctiventris*, which can show as early as June 1. Both species have peak emergences in May and June, and again in September and October.

Baetis tricaudatus emerges on every trout stream in this area and is often the most abundant mayfly on a given stream. Larger trout frequently feed on nymphs and crippled or knocked-down duns of this species.

FIGURE 17 – *BAETIS* NYMPH

FIGURE 18 – *BAETIS* DUN

Both species are small: #18 through #22. A wide variety of dun and nymph colors may be observed, but olive and grayish olive are most common. All stages have two tails.

Emergences occur in the afternoon, typically 1 to 4 P.M. The best hatches occur on cloudy, cool days. Bright, warm conditions mean a short, sporadic emergence.

Baetis tricaudatus hatches can be so heavy that your fly may have a difficult time competing with the naturals. Fish get so locked into and confident taking nymphs that one may take your nymph, hook himself, and continue to feed, as long as you don't put pressure on him.

For both emergences use crippled, knocked-down dun patterns. *Baetis tricaudatus* spinners are not important to anglers. They are rarely seen.

Baetis punctiventris duns and spinners are significant on only two local rivers—the Madison and Firehole, both in Yellowstone Park. The nymphs of this species are not important to anglers. The overriding consideration in fishing B. *punctiventris* duns or spinners is current speed. While they emerge on all areas of both rivers, fish will only feed on them where it is beneficial to do so. Fish never expend more energy feeding than they gain from doing so. Smooth, moderate, or slow flows are thus required, or the naturals will be ignored.

Look for our first tiny blue-winged olive, the *Baetis tricaudatus*, to appear on the Firehole from opening day in late May to the first of July, and again from September through the end of the fishing season. The same holds true for the Madison River in the Park. On the Madison River below Earthquake Lake watch for the emergence from May to mid-June, and again from September 1 through October. Slough Creek's emergences begin in July and go through the end of the season, as do the Yellowstone River's *Baetis* hatches. On the Henry's Fork this hatch can start as early as April and last into early November. The Gallatin River can have good emergences from May through October, depending on conditions.

The *Baetis punctiventris* emerges on the Firehole all year, with peaks in May and June and again in September and October. On the Madison in Yellowstone Park look for this mayfly in June and again in September and October.

Good fly patterns for fishing tiny blue-winged olives are #18–22 Pheasant Tail and Baetis Nymphs, #20–22 Baetis Emergers, #18–22 Baetis Sparkle Duns, #18–22 Baetis Knocked Down Duns, and #20–22 Baetis Spinners.

Early Light Olive Duns—Rhithrogena *Species*

The first large mayfly of the season is present on the rivers like Henry's Fork in Idaho and the Madison, Yellowstone, and Gallatin in Montana. Spinner stages of two *Rhithrogena* mayflies can be important on Montana's Gallatin and Madison Rivers. The Yellowstone River in the Park sees fine spinner activity, also.

Early season hatches of this mayfly occur on the Henry's Fork in mid-April, and on the Madison, Yellowstone, and lower Gallatin in mid-May and continue to mid-June. Both duns and spinners will be on the water at the same time, and fish will rise to both stages.

FIGURE 19 – EARLY LIGHT OLIVE DUN

Duns are large—#14 or #16—with pale olive bodies and dun-colored wings that have dark venation. Both duns and spinners are two-tailed.

Spinners are reddish brown with the typically clear wings of most mayfly spinners. You'll often observe spinners swarming over the riverbanks in the morning prior to mating and egg laying.

Fish seem to ignore the nymphs.

On the Madison, Gallatin, and Yellowstone, summer emerges of *Rhithrogena* can be important, too.

Good fly patterns for fishing early light olives are #14–16 Rhithrogena Emergers, #16 Olive Sparkle Duns, and #14–16 Rusty Sparkle Spinners.

Pale Morning Duns—Ephemerella infrequens *and* E. inermis

The pale morning dun, or PMD, is certainly the most important mayfly in the West. These lovely mayflies inhabit every trout

FIGURE 20 – PALE MORNING NYMPH

stream and are a major hatch on most. Each phase of their life cycle is fed on heavily by trout. Anyone expecting to fish Yellowstone country during the summer should know this insect.

Both species look and act alike, so I will treat them as one. Most nymphs range in color from amber to chocolate brown, #14 through #20. Duns are bright green to orange and yellowish olive, and also #14 through #20. Their wings can range from the same color as that of the dun's body to a light gray. PMD spinner wings are always clear, but the body color can range from rust to light olive and yellow, #16 through #20. Nymphs, duns, and spinners all have three tails.

The nymphs are readily taken by trout. As they ascend to the surface and drift in the film prior to emergence, they are easily recognized and very available to trout. Larger trout may feed only on these drifting nymphs during emergences.

Crippled and deformed duns are common during the heavy hatches of this insect. Trout recognize this vulnerability and often feed exclusively on them. Frequently, too, fully emerged duns ride the surface for long distances, giving fish a prolonged opportunity to feed on them.

Spinners can also be important for anglers and trout. Usually they fall in the morning and evening.

PMD activity is both predictable and consistent. During their predicted activity you can always count on PMDs if the weather conditions are proper. And generally, they emerge at the most comfortable time of the day. On Yellowstone Park's Firehole and stretches of the Madison during June, this means around noon. On a hot July day on the Henry's Fork look for them to show at 9 A.M. Emergences usually last for an hour or two. When "perfect" weather conditions occur—snow or misting rain—I have fished PMD emergences beginning at 11 A.M. and lasting until 6 P.M., with wave after wave of emerging PMDs coming off the Firehole River. Fish rose and snow fell until, mercifully, a dark cold settled in and the fish quit so I could go back to the truck and warm up late in the afternoon.

Expect spinner falls on warm, calm mornings and evenings—usually from 9 A.M. to noon and again from 7 P.M. to dark (which may be as late as 10 P.M. during PMD time).

Larger fish tend to prefer nymphs or crippled duns. Use of a floating PMD nymph and another that sinks a few inches below the film is required, as is a dun pattern tied trapped in its shuck, such as a Sparkle Dun. Trout recognize crippled duns and almost always take an imitation of one whether they are rising to fully emerged or to impaired natural duns.

It may be hard, but it's usually necessary to determine whether rising fish are taking nymphs, emergers, or duns. Most often, larger fish will be selective to one stage. If you see duns drift over trout and the trout take them, then obviously you can assume that they prefer duns. If you see noses, heads, and backs breaking the surface, you can also bet that these risers are working duns. If fish let duns pass by, however, then look to nymphs. If you see trout tails, nymphs are being taken.

During PMD spinner falls trout can be tough to take. Often, rising trout seem to lock onto a spinner of a particular color. Quite often a pale olive imitation is best.

PMDs emerge on Yellowstone Park's Firehole and Madison Rivers from the opening day of fishing season until July 8; on the Park's Slough Creek from July 1 to 20; and on the Yellowstone River from July 15 to September 5. On the Henry's Fork look to June 1 through the month of July for PMD activity. On Montana's Madison River PMDs often emerge from the end of June to mid-August.

Good fly patterns for fishing pale morning duns are #14–20 Pheasant Tails and PMD Nymphs, #16–20 PMD Emergers, and #14–20 PMD Sparkle Duns, Knocked Down Duns, No-Hackles, and Sparkle and Foam Spinners.

Western Green Drakes—Drunella grandis, D. doddsi, and D. coloradensis, and Timpanoga hecuba

While the Henry's Fork has perhaps the best population of green drakes, many other rivers in this area also offer outstanding

FIGURE 21 – GREEN DRAKE NYMPH

opportunities to meet and fish this mayfly. The Lamar, Yellowstone, Gallatin, and Madison Rivers, along with Slough and Soda Butte Creeks, all experience fine green drake emergences.

Four mayfly species are grouped under this heading. Although closely related, these different species vary in appearance and emergence dates.

The dun stage of the green drake is the most important for fly fishers. Depending on the species, duns range from olive to yellow to brown. Nymph, dun, and spinner all have three tails and run from #8 through #12.

While nymphs of this mayfly may take trout, they are not important. And while spinners are usually insignificant due to their habit of falling during the early-morning hours when it's still dark, we have encountered a few spinner falls over the past several years that have brought up big trout. During the summers of 1995 and 1996, for example, several spinner falls occurred from 8 to 10 A.M., producing fine dry-fly activity.

Emergences begin around 10 A.M. During the first few days of a hatch the trout may seem suspicious of the large duns, but once they get onto them it takes only a few such duns to bring the fish to the surface. And for several days following an emergence trout will recognize the big duns and come up for imitations even when no naturals are emerging.

During heavy hatches trout often allow fully emerged duns to pass by, instead taking floating nymphs and crippled and emerging duns. During sparse activity trout invariably rise for any drake that passes. The emerger pattern has always been a favorite. It's seldom refused.

Look for this activity on the Henry's Fork from mid-June to July 6; the Park's Yellowstone River from the middle to the end of July; the Lamar River and Slough Creek from late August through September.

Good fly patterns for fishing the green drakes are #10–12 Green Drake Emergers, #12 Green Drake and Drake Mackerel Sparkle Duns, and #10–12 Green Drake Spinners.

Big Brown Drakes—Ephemera simulans

This enormous mayfly brings up gargantuan fish on the two rivers it inhabits in fishable numbers in Yellowstone country—the Henry's Fork and Gibbon Rivers.

Emergences take place during late June and into early July from 7 to 10 P.M. Spinner falls often coincide with emergences.

Nymphs vary in color from tan to dark brown. All stages of this mayfly have three tails. The nymphs are able swimmers, so imitations of nymphs must be moved with short, rapid pulls. Rises to nymphs are most often aggressive, leaving a big swirl at the surface.

On the Gibbon River fish rise to crippled duns and spinners. On the Henry's Fork a nymph is often required. Here, trout will often rise once, then move several feet and work again.

Carry nymphs, emergers, and duns and try them all on the Henry's Fork. For the Gibbon, a Sparkle Dun or spinner pattern works fine.

ON MIDGE

FLYING ANT

E RIBBON FOAM BEETLE

DAVE'S HOPPER

WOOLHEAD SCULPIN

NATURE STONEFLY NYMPH (MATURE)

STIMULATOR

LITTLE YELLOW STONEFLY

DAMSEL NYMPH

SERENDIPITY

ONTAINE SPARKLE PUPA

TAN IMPROVED X CADDIS

E CADDIS

SPENT SPARKLE CADDIS

GREEN CADDIS LARVA

PHEASANT-TAIL NYMPH

PALE MORNING SPARKLE DUN

DRAKE MACKERAL EMERGER

FLAV KNOCKED-DOWN DUN

GRAY DRAKE FOAM SPINNER

FIGURE 22 – BROWN DRAKE SPINNER

Duns and spinners are usually a full #8, and they both have heavily mottled wings. Their bodies are light brown with darker rings.

Look for emergences on the Gibbon and Henry's Fork from June 20 to mid-July.

Good fly patterns for fishing the brown drake are #8–10 Brown Drake Nymphs, Sparkle Duns, and Foam Spinners.

Small Western Green Drakes—Drunella flavilinea

You know it's time for the small western green drake hatch in Yellowstone country when the "Fraternal Order of the Flavilinea" cruises into West Yellowstone. This is a group of noble fly fishers led by Lew Terwilliger who come to this area every spring to fish this hatch on their beloved Firehole River. No group of anglers knows more about a river or single mayfly emergence.

This group will explain that "flavs," as they are commonly called, are found not only on the Firehole but also on the Yellowstone River in the Park. Look for them, too, on the Henry's Fork in Idaho and the Madison below Earthquake Lake in Montana.

FIGURE 23 – FLAV NYMPH

FIGURE 24 – FLAV SPINNER

Depending on the weather, you can expect these olive mayflies to emerge anytime between 3 and 10 P.M. On sunny days they won't show up until sunset, which is usually between 8 and 10 P.M. from mid-June into July. In cloudy conditions they should show between 5 and 6 P.M.

As with most mayfly emergences, inclement weather seems to produce the heaviest hatches, biggest rises of trout, and best fishing. Last June the Fraternal Flavs saw a late-afternoon weather front moving into the lower geyser basin area of the Firehole. The group had just left Lost Glasses Pool and moved up to the parking area below Plunge Pool. They sat inside their vehicle, enjoying the car's heater while waiting for the cold front to pass and the sleet to let up a bit. Lew got his troops fired up by explaining that they might see a flav emergence at Plunge Pool, since the weather was so favorable. Upriver they trudged against the north wind and rain, passing several anglers who had already spent the afternoon on the river. Everyone else was calling it a day, due to the weather.

At the pool several fish were already working #14 and #16 olive-bodied duns. A great time was had by all fishing emergers and Sparkle Duns on the surface before the sky opened up, releasing a tremendous downpour of rain mixed with snow and driving the group to town.

For this emergence a nymph is seldom required, because fish generally rise to impaired or fully emerged duns. Nymphs, duns, and spinners all have three tails.

The Firehole River flavs emerge during the first three weeks of June. On the Yellowstone in the Park look for them from mid-July to mid-August. On the Madison below Earthquake Lake flavs emerge during this same time. On the Henry's Fork look for flavs from June 25 to July 25.

Good fly patterns for fishing the flavs are #14–16 Flav Sparkle Duns, Knocked Down Duns, No-Hackles, and Sparkle Spinners.

Gray Drakes—Siphlonurus occidentalis
A large mayfly, the gray drake is found in streams, rivers, and one lake in this area. This #10 pale olive to tan and light brown

mayfly is unmistakable. Notice the dark brown horseshoe markings at the rear of each body segment on the belly of a dun or spinner.

The only situation in which I have found these three-tailed nymphs important is when I'm fishing to visible cruising trout on Yellowstone Lake. Such trout search the shoreline for gray drake nymphs that have migrated there to emerge. For an imitation, I tie a simple thin-bodied Hare's Ear pattern.

Because the nymphs crawl out of the water and the duns often emerge on shore, many anglers do not tie dun patterns. Often, however, when I present a Gray Drake Sparkle Dun to rising fish, they take it. Even though duns are seldom available to trout, due to their emergence behavior, trout recognize a trailing shuck as the sign of a crippled dun trapped at the surface film, and they will rise readily to such an imitation. Duns and spinners both sport two tails.

Spinner falls provide concentrated activity and lots of rising trout daily from 10 A.M. to 1 P.M. If warm and calm conditions prevail in the evening, a spinner fall may occur then, too—from 7 P.M.

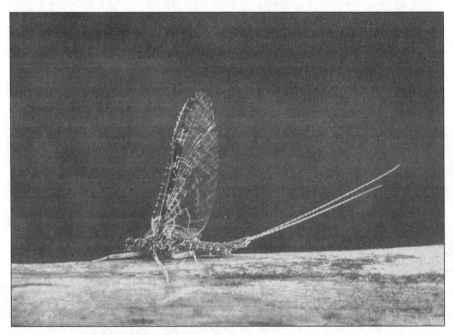

FIGURE 25 – SPECKLED-WINGED SPINNER

to dark. Spinners are tan with the aforementioned dark brown horseshoe markings on their bellies. Because of the large size of this fly, some fish can be extremely shy about taking spinners. The take is often slow and deliberate, so be careful when striking. Let the fish rise and turn away before you strike; and do so slowly, to protect a light tippet.

Gray drakes appear on the Madison River in the park June 10 to early July; on Slough Creek during July, August, and into September; on the Yellowstone River from mid-July to mid-September; on Yellowstone Lake during July and early August; and on the Henry's Fork from June 20 into mid-July.

Good fly patterns for fishing gray drakes are #10 Gray Drake Nymphs, Sparkle Duns, and Gray Drake Foam Spinners.

Speckled-Winged Spinners—Callibaetis americanus

A mayfly of the stillwaters and weed beds, this lovely insect is responsible for many gulpers rising on lakes, ponds, and sloughs.

The #14 or #16 nymph, dun, and spinner stages are all relished by trout. The three-tailed nymph inhabits weed beds. It is a streamlined, tannish gray insect that often darts about in short spurts. Duns range in color from pale olive to tan, and they always have distinctly mottled gray and brown wings. Spinners resemble duns but have much longer tails and clear wings mottled heavily with brown. Both duns and spinners have two tails.

The duns begin emerging around 10 A.M. and may continue until 2 P.M. if conditions allow. Look for spinners to fall at about the same time or later. Trout seldom show a preference for either stage.

Note that if the wind is stronger than a breeze and producing a good chop on lakes before expected *Callibaetis* activity, then—no matter how heavy the emergence or spinner fall—trout will fail to rise to the insects on the water.

This mayfly produces fine activity on most lakes in Yellowstone country. I have fished trout rising to its duns and spinners on Hebgen and Earthquake Lakes in May, and during its next brood from early July into September. On Hidden and Ennis Lakes I have had good action from the middle of June into July. On lakes such as Grebe, Trout, and Cascade in the Park, look for speckled-winged spinners to appear anytime from late June through mid-September. On sloughs and ponds big trout cruise for nymphs, duns, and spinners during this same time. On the Henry's Fork look for *Callibaetis* in slow stretches of water on the lower Railroad Ranch during August and early September.

Good fly patterns for fishing speckled-winged spinners are #14–16 Callibaetis Nymphs, Sparkle Duns, and Foam Spinners.

Tricos—Tricorythodes *Species*

Only two rivers and one lake in my home area produce fishable hatches of this little white-winged mayfly. However, other rivers—such as the Bighorn and Missouri—offer outstanding dry-fly fishing to huge pods of rising trout during trico activity.

Over the seasons many local anglers have witnessed tremendous rises of fish to tricos on the Madison River from its mouth at Hebgen Lake upstream to Barns Pools in Yellowstone Park. While most of these risers are whitefish, some trout up from the lake are working, too. Those in the know take many fine rainbow and brown

FIGURE 26 – TRICO ADULT

trout during this activity. They locate rising trout and present their dun patterns only to these trout, rather than shotgunning their casts into pods of whitefish and hoping for a trout.

Tricos may vary widely in size. On the Madison River and Hebgen Lake females can run as large as #18. On the Henry's Fork mostly #22s will be encountered. Also, nymphs can be important on the Henry's Fork, while on the Madison River and Hebgen Lake they are not a factor, because the trout prefer duns or spinners. Nymphs, duns, and spinners all have three tails.

Nymphs are #20 or #22, dark chocolate brown in color, and available to trout only on their emergence. Male duns are always smaller than females. Males are black, #22. Females on Hebgen Lake and the Madison River are #18 and have olive bodies. Female duns are readily taken on the Madison Arm of Hebgen Lake from 6 to 9 A.M., and only during calm conditions—any wave action and the jig is up. Here, spinners are rarely important. The only time fish might rise to them is in areas where the current has gathered several together. I've seen trout rise to clumps of trico spinners, and I've taken fish using a Griffith's Gnat to imitate such clumps.

On the Madison River and Henry's Fork, spinner falls provide outstanding midmorning rises. On the Fork you must be prepared to fish all stages—nymph, dun, and spinner.

You will find tricos on Hebgen Lake from mid-June through August. On the Madison River above the lake and on the Henry's Fork look for them from the middle of July to mid-September.

Good fly patterns for fishing tricos are #20 Chocolate Brown Fur Nymphs, #18 Olive Sparkle Duns, and #20–22 Trico Sparkle Duns and Spinners.

Pink Ladies—Epeorus albertae

The name of this impressive mayfly is derived from the body color of the female dun and spinner. Males have pale olive bodies, and both sexes have light gray wings. The wings of spinners are always clear. Nymphs and adults range from #14 to #16 and are two-tailed.

FIGURE 27 – PINK LADY DUN

Because these mayflies shed their nymphal shucks near the stream bottom and rise to the surface as fully formed duns, the only insects to reach the surface are perfectly formed. Cripples or partially emerged duns never make it. This is a behavior unique to the pink lady. Still, despite the fact that trout only feed on perfect duns at the surface, a Sparkle Dun or emerger pattern is very effective. During an emergence of this mayfly trout feed either exclusively on the surface or exclusively subsurface. Never will you see them switch from on e to the other during an emergence. Most likely the fish will recognize and take an emerger regardless of where in the water column you fish it.

Spinner falls are sometimes heavy on rivers like the Madison. The females lay their eggs and drop spent onto the surface as darkness falls. Then large trout key on the spinners, sipping them in the pickets and along the shoreline well after dark. I like to use a spinner pattern that is easy to see in failing light, one with a double wing of bright white zelon like the Pink Lady Spinner.

On the Park's smooth-flowing Yellowstone look for emergences to occur during August. On heavy waters such as the Madison, Gallatin, and Gardner you can often encounter pink ladies during July and August.

Good fly patterns for fishing pink ladies are #14–16 Pink Lady Emergers, Sparkle Duns, and No-Hackles.

Margaritas—Attenella margarita—Late-Summer Olives

Every September parades of anglers tell of their disappointment at fishing a great morning mayfly emergence on the Yellowstone River near Buffalo Ford. They report that they saw hundreds of rising trout and a surface covered with little olive mayflies but were unable to fool a single riser. This mayfly emergence frustrates anglers because they do not patiently observe what the trout are feeding on. Thus this hatch, and others, teaches an important lesson: The presence of adults on the surface does not always mean that rising trout are feeding on them.

With this and many other hatches, what appears to be fish rising to adults is really trout taking nymphs at the surface.

The margarita emergence can be especially frustrating, though. Often trout will take one nymph at the surface, then go

FIGURE 28 – MARGARITA DUN

under to take several more before moving and rising again. So what looks like a few fish rising may actually be many fish feeding heavily underneath and occasionally rising to the surface.

Because fish feed largely beneath the surface and move so much while they feed on this mayfly, it's imperative that you fish only to visible trout.

Yellowstone River cutthroats prefer nymphs during this mayfly hatch, but the duns experience many emergence defects, making a crippled pattern necessary at times. Spinners can also be important during their evening and morning falls, which occur in calm, warm conditions.

The nymph of this species ranges from amber to dark brown, always #18. Duns are olive to olive-brown and have medium gray wings. The spinners are olive with clear wings. All stages have three tails.

The Yellowstone River is home to this mayfly from mid-August to early October.

Good fly patterns for fishing late-summer olives are #18 Margarita Fur Nymphs, Pheasant Tail Nymphs, Sparkle Duns, and Olive Spinners.

Late-Season Brown-Olive Duns—Serratella tibialis
      This mayfly often appears with its cousin the late-season olive, *Attenella margarita*, on the Yellowstone during August and September. This #16 mayfly may present the same scenario to fly fishers as the margarita—ascending nymphs being taken over fully emerged duns. Trout sometimes show a preference for the nymphs, because they can easily take these nymphs and are suspicious of any floating fly this late in the season.

When both species are on the water at the same time you must determine which one is preferred. Cutthroats do pick one over the other despite their similarities.

It's also very important to observe closely and seine the water to determine which stage the trout are rising to. If they are taking duns on the surface, then long fine leaders and 6X tippets are in

FIGURE 29 – LATE-SEASON OLIVE DUN

FIGURE 30 – LATE-SEASON OLIVE SPINNER

order. Your pattern should be a cripple with a trailing shuck, due to the emergence problems that this species often has.

If trout are taking nymphs, however, then work to a visible fish, presenting your nymph at the same level at which he is taking naturals.

Emergences of this mayfly come off best on cool, cloudy days from 11 A.M. to 3 P.M. Spinner falls are frequently seen on warm, calm evenings.

All stages of the brown-olive dun are three-tailed. Since the natural nymphs vary widely in color from yellow to brown, the color of an imitation is never critical. Still, a brown nymph is best. The duns are brownish olive with dark slate wings; spinners are olive.

Look to the Yellowstone River to provide this mayfly emergence from mid-August through September.

Good fly patterns for fishing the late-season brown-olive duns are #16 Brown Fur Nymphs, Pheasant Tail Nymphs, and Olive Sparkle Duns and Spinners.

Mahogany Duns—Paraleptophlebia bicornuta *and* P. debilis
Some of the season's last rises of trout to emerging mayflies come during our fall hatches of mahogany duns. While several species emerge during the summer months, these two fall species are the most significant to fly fishers. I have fished good emergences of this mayfly on the Henry's Fork and Gibbon Rivers.

On the Fork this mayfly may emerge concurrently with tricos. Here, the big rainbows will often key on the larger mahogany duns even though they're far less numerous. On the Gibbon I have fished fine hatches when a rainstorm moved in, spoiling my terrestrial action but providing perfect mayfly weather.

Most larger trout prefer to rise to nymphs in the surface film. The three-tailed, dark brown #16 nymphs are fair swimmers. Seldom will you locate a sizable rising trout that prefers duns. Even long after an emergence is over I have had good success presenting a floating nymph in likely looking holds on the Gibbon and Henry's

FIGURE 31 – MAHOGANY DUN

Fork. If you do find a trout rising only to emerged duns, give him a dark brown Sparkle Dun.

The duns emerge around 10 A.M. and may continue until 2 P.M. They are three-tailed and seldom emerge in any concentration, yet trout relish this mayfly even when it's present in small numbers.

Spinners may be seen in the morning, though seldom in the numbers that prompt fish selectivity to a specific pattern. A rusty or dark brown #16 spinner will work.

On the Gibbon River's Meadows and Elk Park sections this mayfly can come off in late August and through September. Henry's Fork emergences are always more consistent and can be expected from mid-August through September. You may encounter sporadic activity on the lower Gallatin River near the mouth of the canyon anytime during late summer.

Good fly patterns for fishing the mahogany duns are #16 Mahogany Fur Nymphs, Sparkle Duns, and Spinners.

Slate/Brown Duns—Heptagenia solitaria

Here is a late-season mayfly emergence that can't be counted on to occur every season—but when it does, it's well worth being prepared for. Some seasons we never see an emergence, but others bring wonderful rises of cutthroats on the Yellowstone River in the Park.

The #14 to #16 duns of this species come off the shallow, slow water along the margins of the river next to shore. Emergences begin around 1 P.M. and may continue until as late as 5 P.M. The big grayish brown, two-tailed duns emerge from their nymphs, which migrate near the shoreline prior to hatching. Any shallow, slow stretch of the river is worth looking at for signs of this emergence. Cutthroats can be found working water only inches deep, searching for crippled *Heptagenia* emergers.

In September the water level on the Yellowstone is low, creating many areas where emergences of this species can be met. Look to the water near Sulphur Cauldron and Buffalo Ford, as well as the slow stretches above LeHardys Rapids, to give up nice emergences.

This mayfly emerges during the late season and in shallow water, and fish do rise to it, though they can be very wary. Be extremely careful with your approach and presentation. A long leader tapered to 6X is required, and a Sparkle Dun presented on a dead drift is the only pattern you need.

The fly pattern for fishing the slate/brown dun is a #16 brown Sparkle Dun.

CADDISFLIES:
THEIR EMERGENCES AND ACTIVITY PERIODS

Caddisflies are as significant as mayflies to western fly fishermen—yet are less understood. This is a shame, because a basic knowledge of their habits is essential for success when fishing western waters during the summer season.

Caddis emergences puzzle most anglers. There are three clues to these hatches on rivers: Trout can be seen leaping out of the water; there are no insects on the water; and most of the rises in the faster currents are bulging and splashy. In slower, moderate flows look for quiet dimples, porpoising rolls, and tails barely breaking the surface. It's important to consider riseforms when deciding what the trout are taking, but it's never wise to make a judgment based solely on them.

Certain caddis offer fly-fishing opportunities when the females return to the water to lay eggs. The following facts will help you recognize egg-laying activity: During it, caddis bounce, skitter, and flutter along the surface, crawl beneath the surface, and float flush in the surface film. You may find spent females on the surface, too.

By learning when and where to expect caddis emergences and how to recognize basic caddis habits, you can be successful during much of the season.

There are only 12 species of caddis responsible for most fly-fishing opportunities in this area. If you only fish certain rivers at certain times of the year, even fewer caddis will be present.

Because caddisflies are so little understood, they have not been given commonly accepted names the way most mayflies have. But since I have to refer to them as something, I've used their Latin names here. Thus, instead of calling a caddis "that little insect with tan wings and a brown body, #16," I'll refer to it by its Latin name.

Brachycentrus occidentalis *and* B. americanus—*Early- and Late-Season Emergers*

The early-season emergence of the *Brachycentrus occidentalis* is often referred to in the Livingston and Bozeman areas as the "Mother's Day caddis," owing to its emergence during early May.

On the Yellowstone River this emergence is often wiped out by heavy spring runoff. The lower Madison near Bozeman offers more reliable fishing: Usually the runoff has not begun before the hatch is well under way.

Early *Brachycentrus* are large. Males are #16, females a full #14. Adults are gray, almost black. An olive stripe is distinctly visible on the sides of their gray abdomens.

FIGURE 32 – *BRACHYCENTRUS* PUPA

FIGURE 33 – *BRACHYCENTRUS* ADULT

Hatches on the Park's Madison and Firehole Rivers are present for the opening day of fishing season in late May and can be expected to continue through the first week in July.

Mother's Day emergences on the Yellowstone and Madison Rivers can be so heavy that a pattern such as the Royal Trude works better than a closer imitation of the natural. The attractor fly gets the trout's attention.

For the emergences on the Madison and Firehole in Yellowstone Park, as well as on the Henry's Fork, adult patterns produce best. These caddis are most active in the afternoon and evening. Also, egg-laying and emergence activities often coincide. When females resurface after diving to lay their eggs, they flop helplessly and drift downstream.

The other *Brachycentrus* emerges late in the summer on the Yellowstone and Henry's Fork. *B. americanus* is lighter gray than the Mother's Day caddis, but otherwise the species look the same. Egg-laying activity for *B. americanus* is the most important stage for anglers. Look for egg layers during cool mornings and evenings or on cloudy afternoons. Watch for fish rising to egg layers behind rocks and logs. Trout will pick off naturals drifting with the currents that have just laid their eggs below the surface. Where no logs or rocks are present female caddis may release their eggs as they skip along on the surface.

The Mother's Day hatch occurs on the Madison and lower Yellowstone from late April to early May. On the Firehole and Madison in the Park look for it from the opening day of fishing season until early July. The Henry's Fork sees this hatch from late May to late June. Be prepared for *Brachycentrus americanus* on the Henry's Fork during mid-August, and on the Yellowstone from late July through August.

Good fly patterns for *Brachycentrus* are #14–16 olive LaFontaine's or Antron Caddis Pupae, and olive X Caddis.

Hydropsyche cockerelli, H. occidentalis, *and* H. placoda

Of all the caddis in Yellowstone country, this is the most important to fly fishers. On the Madison's 40-mile blue-ribbon stretch, from Earthquake Lake to Ennis, no other insect comes close to this one for providing continuous fly-fishing opportunities.

From June to mid-August during the late evening you'll see thousands of these caddis over the surface of the river. Adults are #14 or #16; they have tan wings and bodies of light brown, golden yellow, or green. Pupae are usually brownish yellow, #14.

Last August Jackie and I took Skip and Carol Morris to a favorite spot on the Madison near the Three Dollar Bridge. We arrived as the sun was setting over the Gravelly Mountains. We sneaked down to a favorite pocket behind some large boulders and waited. Soon a few smaller trout begin rising out in the faster currents, splashing and bulging after emerging *Hydropsyche*. It was tempting to begin casting to the risers but we held off, knowing that the larger browns and rainbows would come later, when darkness set in. And by patiently waiting and not disturbing the water, we were able to see the entire emergence unfold. At dark, the quiet water near the shore came alive with subtle dimples and tails barely breaking the surface. The big trout were rising to emerging *Hydropsyche* caddis.

FIGURE 34 – *HYDROPSYCHE* ADULT

Skip took his turn first, because Carol wanted a picture of him with a nice trout. He indeed took a fine rainbow after giving an Irise Caddis pupa a short, drag-free presentation. Next it was Carol's turn, and she decided to try casting an X Caddis pattern to a big bank-sipping brown. I've since sent them a photo I took of her with the largest brown she'd ever caught. The moon was just clearing Sheep Mountain in the background when we left rising trout—at almost 11 P.M.!

The emergence is the period you want to fish during this all-important caddis activity. As trout take emerging caddis pupae their feeding rhythms and riseforms change. Tails and dorsal fins break the surface as the fish take the pupae just beneath it. Rises of worthwhile fish are slow and deliberate. Smaller fish aggressively pursue pupae and rocket into the air after them.

Even though trout rise mostly to the pupae, you don't always have to fish one. An Irise or X Caddis, imitating an emerging caddis stuck in its shuck, is most productive. These patterns are always fished dry and often work better than pupa imitations.

On the Madison River look for this caddis to show from early June to mid-August; on the Firehole from the season opener in late May to mid-October; on the Yellowstone from opening day on July 15 to mid-August. The Henry's Fork's *Hydropsyche* can be fished from mid-May through June.

Fly patterns for *Hydropsyche* are #14–16 tan LaFontaine's and Antron Caddis Pupae, and tan Irise Caddis, X Caddis, and Elkhair Caddis.

Helicopsyche borealis—*Spring-Creek Caddis*
This particular caddis can give you fits if you're not prepared to match its small size. While most emergences are found on the Firehole and Henry's Fork, these caddis are also found on some of the area's spring creeks.

The *H. borealis* is the only species of *Helicopsyche* found in Yellowstone country. It is a tiny #20 with dark gray wings and a body the lovely amber color of good Scotch whiskey. During egg-laying activity the naturals are available to trout in great numbers on the Firehole River. On the Henry's Fork and some area spring creeks it's possible to fish emergences of this caddis as well as its egg-laying activity.

Trout feed on these caddis during cool afternoons, as well as during warm evenings, when the females crawl from grassy banks at the water's surface to lay their eggs. All that's required for trout to feed on these tiny caddis is water deep enough to make fish feel secure and a current speed that makes it worth their effort. Sections of the Firehole and area spring creeks see fine rises to these caddis.

On spring creeks and the Henry's Fork, look for these caddis to emerge in the evening. It may be tough to discern whether trout are rising to this species or to one of the other caddis species that are usually present. Here you must use your seine and your patience.

Egg layers may use bank vegetation or simply jump off the streamside grass into the water to lay their eggs. Once on the water they will ride the surface for long distances. Fishing is restricted to the banks. You must walk and search for rising trout working the egg-laying females.

On the Firehole and spring creeks look for this caddisfly to appear from mid-June to mid-July. On the Henry's Fork the tiny caddis shows from mid-May to early July.

Good fly patterns for fishing the *Helicopsyche* are #20 amber Antron Caddis Pupae and gray X Caddis.

Glossosoma montana

The tiny *Glossosoma montana* has sporadic emergences, yet the fly is often important to fly fishers.

This is the smallest caddis valuable to western anglers. It's true that the #20 gray-bodied and gray-winged insects are tough to pre-dict, and that their emergences vary in importance from year to year. Still, you should always carry a few imitations of *Glossosoma montana* pupae. Their July emergences on the Madison River have overshadowed *Hydropsyche* caddis hatches many times. This has also occurred on the Henry's Fork and Firehole.

FIGURE 35 – *GLOSSOSOMA MONTANA*

On the Madison River look for this emergence in July. On the Henry's Fork sporadic activity may be observed from June to early September. The Firehole sees this caddis sporadically from late June through September.

Good fly patterns for *Glossosoma* are #20 black LaFontaine's and Antron Caddis Pupae, and #20 black X Caddis.

Oecetis disjuncta—*Longhorn Sedges*

Anglers cannot mistake the long antennae of the longhorn sedge—another caddis of spring creeks and, sometimes, the Madison River. Its body ranges from golden yellow to bright green, and its wings are light gray to tan. The antennae are always long—two to three times the wing length. Adults are usually #16.

This caddisfly is important during its dramatic egg-laying period. Look for them during late afternoon and evening, especially spent naturals.

Spent longhorn sedge caddis patterns are usually the only patterns required for this emergence and subsequent egg-laying activity.

FIGURE 36 – LONGHORN SEDGE

Trout seem to remember the distinct profiles of these caddis and rise to them whenever the opportunity arises.

Look for longhorns on area spring creeks, the Henry's Fork, and the Gibbon River from mid-June to the first week of July. On the Madison hatching activity is sporadic, but when it occurs this caddis species provides outstanding fishing during the last two weeks of July.

Good fly patterns for *Oecetis* are #14–16 green Irise Caddis, Spent Sparkle Caddis, and G & H Sedges.

Cheumatopsyche pettiti *and* C. lasia—*the Daytime-Emerging Caddis*

Beginning in mid-June and lasting into August, a #18 olive-bodied, brown-winged caddis emerges. Upon hatching, the adult rides the water farther than any other caddis species. Its emergence is the only time the *Cheumatopsyche* caddis seems to be important. Trout rise to adult patterns as well as pupae.

Emergences take place at all times of the day—as long as it's cloudy. While the hatch is never heavy or regular, it doesn't take many adults to get trout rising. Often this caddis emerges prior to pale morning dun or *Baetis* mayflies during optimal weather conditions for mayfly emergences. This is a real bonus if you're prepared to meet and fish the emergence of this fine caddisfly species.

Look for emergences on the Henry's Fork from mid-June to the first week in August.

Good fly patterns for *Cheumatopsyche* are #18 olive LaFontaine's and Antron Caddis Pupae, and #18 olive X Caddis.

The Long-Emerging Lepidostoma pluviale

You may encounter emergences of this caddis from the middle of June to mid-September. The females are #18, with olive bodies and brown wings. Males are similar in color but also have distinct dark gray recurves on the leading edges of their wings.

This classic little caddis emerges in the evening. Trout rise to both adults and pupae. Often you can watch the adults riding the currents for several seconds after emerging. Trout will rise to adult patterns fished during emergences, but larger fish prefer pupal patterns. The emergences are often heavy, bringing on big rises of trout.

FIGURE 37 – *LEPIDOSTOMA* ADULT

Egg laying also prompts rises to this species. During this period caddis will ride the surface passively during the afternoon and into the evening. It's important here to seine the water to determine whether trout are rising to emerging pupae or to egg-laying adults. An imitation of the adult is likely to take trout more easily, which can make this caddis one of the easiest to fish. However, larger trout are selective to the pupa, so it pays to be aware of the individual preference of each trout.

Look for emergence to begin on the Henry's Fork in mid-June and last to mid-July. On the Madison River and area spring creeks it can be expected from mid-July until mid-August. Slough Creek's activity begins around July 4 and lasts through August, while the Yellowstone River's hatch can last from its opening day in the Park until Labor Day.

Good fly patterns for *Lepidostoma* are #18 olive LaFontaine's and Antron Caddis Pupae, #18 X Caddis, and #18 Spent Sparkle Caddis.

The big, sprinting Arctopsyche grandis

At #8 to #10, this is the largest caddis to emerge in quantity on the Madison River. *Arctopsyche grandis* adult behavior involves running about madly on streamside boulders, covering lots of country but really going nowhere.

This species is largely nocturnal, and only adult and larva imitations are important to anglers. Both can be fine searching patterns for heavy water. To eliminate crowding problems the larvae move about in response to water fluctuations and population densities. Trout relish the big, juicy larvae, which vary in color from a chromatic green on the Madison River to brownish olive on the Gallatin. Because the larvae move so much, trout can easily recognize them as a fine meal, and they take imitations readily.

On the Madison it's common to see many *Arctopsyche grandis* adults running the banks on cloudy afternoons. Due to the large number of naturals and their size you'd expect heavy emergences and egg-laying flights, with big numbers of rising trout. In reality

FIGURE 38 – *ARCTOPSYCHE GRANDIS*

you won't see either an emergence or an egg-laying flight—or trout feeding exclusively on either stage. It's my hunch that both the emergence and egg-laying flight are nocturnal. Still, it is important to recognize the adults, and to know when they are running the banks. When no other insect activity is evident, imitating an adult or larva of this insect can produce fine action.

Look for the bright green- to dirty olive-bodied adults with mottled brown wings to show on the Madison River anytime from late June through July. On the Gallatin River you should encounter them during the entire month of July.

Good fly patterns for the *Arctopsyche* are #10 bright green Caddis Larvae and #10 olive X Caddis.

Hesperophylax designatus *of the Yellowstone River*

When this big, yellow/ginger-winged caddis is laying eggs on the smooth stretches of Yellowstone River in the Park, anglers often confuse it with the golden stonefly.

Hesperophylax designatus adults are a large #8 and when seen flying in the distance are easy to mistake for golden stoneflies.

FIGURE 39 – *HESPEROPHYLAX DESIGNATUS*

Their bodies are always a brilliant olive. The yellow/ginger wings are divided down the middle by a distinct black and white stripe.

Egg-laying activity brings on fine rises of cutthroats, even though you will never see heavy concentrations of this caddis. Its size alone makes it important. Adults will be taken whenever they are on the water. The trout know what they are and go out of their way to intercept them.

Egg-laying females can often be seen from late morning to early afternoon skittering along the shoreline, laying their eggs. Often you can do well by dragging a golden stone imitation, such as a Stimulator or Elkhair Caddis, along the shoreline, imitating the movement of these females.

Look for this species on the Yellowstone from the season opener in mid-July until early August.

Good fly patterns for *Hesperophylax* are #8–10 Elkhair Caddis, Kaufmann Stimulators, and Golden Stone Adults.

Rhyacophila bifila *and* R. coloradensis—*the Cro-magnon Caddis*

In caddisfly evolution advancement is measured in part by the ability to build protective housing for larvae. That refinement is lacking in this species. *Rhyacophila* larvae freely roam about the bottom of western trout streams without the cases of sticks and stones used by other species. Partly because of this feature, the "caddis green" larvae of this caddis are more important to anglers than the adults.

These caddis are found in the turbulent pocket water of many western trout streams. A larva imitation is one of the most useful searching flies you can have. The mature naturals are available to trout from early summer to late fall.

Adults of both species range in size from #14 to #16—as do the larvae. Adults exhibit a lovely olive body and mottled gray and black wings.

FIGURE 40 – CRO-MAGNON CADDIS

During September, I have experienced fine fishing with adult patterns whenever I can find a trout rising to the sporadic egg-laying activity that this species provides.

My friend Dr. Charlie Cummings and I were fishing grasshoppers on the Madison River near the Grizzly Bar one early-September day a few years back. After lunch cumulus clouds built up, shading the bright sunlight so important in getting hopper action going during the late season. So Charlie and I were sitting on the bank chatting about bird dogs and shooting when a few trout began rising. They turned out to be taking ovipositing *Rhyacophila* females that were dancing about in the heavier flows. At first only smaller fish came slashing after the egg layers. But shortly, larger trout began taking the naturals drifting calmly in the quieter water near shore. We took turns presenting our adult patterns to the larger calm-water bankside risers, leaving the aggressive smaller fish alone in the heavier currents. It was an important lesson we learned that afternoon—one that can pay off during any *Rhyacophila* egg laying.

Look for the early species, *Rhyacophila bifila*, on the Madison during July and August. Use larva imitations. On the Yellowstone this same activity occurs from mid- to late August, when adults can be important. The same is true for the Gallatin during July and August. The later species, *R. coloradensis*, provides both larva and adult activity on the Madison and Firehole during September and October.

Good fly patterns for *Rhyacophila* are #14–16 Caddis Green Larvae, #14–16 olive X Caddis, and #16 Hemingway Caddis.

Micrasema bactro

During the short span of three weeks this caddisfly may be seen on the Park's Yellowstone River, but it usually offers fishermen only a week of activity. On the few evenings that they're active, these caddis appear in tremendous numbers, becoming the most significant insect on the water.

The #20 adults have bright green bodies and black wings. Whether these caddis are laying eggs or emerging, trout love them.

FIGURE 41 – *MICRASEMA BACTRO*

When other caddis species and insects are on the water at the same time that this caddis is emerging, you may have a problem determining the preference of rising trout. The odds are usually against risers working *Micrasema*, though, because they are on the water only one week all season. Still, if your seine reveals *Micrasema* pupae, suspect them of causing the activity, because they will outnumber other insects during their few emergence dates.

Egg-laying activity is an easy call. Many times you will feel rather than see the clue to *Micrasema* egg laying. The tiny caddis sometimes deposit their gooey green egg clusters right on your waders. Cutthroat trout relish the egg layers so much that they will bump and push them off your leg!

This caddisfly can be fished from mid-July through the first week of August during those rare times when you come upon its activity. Be prepared.

Good fly patterns for *Micrasema* are #20 green Antron Pupae, Yellowstone Irise Caddis, green X Caddis, and Spent Sparkle Caddis.

Mystacides alafimbriata

This #16 dark caddis provides fine dry-fly fishing during the late summer on the Henry's Fork and some spring creeks. The caddis are usually active from 7 to 10 A.M., mid-July through August. Adults may be seen dancing above the surface or riding the water close to the banks.

Nick Lyons and I were at the slow, silty stretch referred to as the "lower pond" on Herb Wellington's private water, a wide piece of water between the crossing and Nick's favorite "Second Bend Pool." Moving like hunters getting close to an alert antelope for a shot, Nick and I eased along the bank trying to approach just below the rising trout. I fully expected to see these bank-sipping browns rising to trico spinners. Their rises seemed much like the casual sips of fish taking spinners from the surface film. We sat and watched, taking note of the dizzying dance being performed by the dark-colored caddis above our bank. One brown was rising not 10 feet above our position, in an indentation along the bank. We watched as he took floating caddis off the surface. Tying on an X Caddis to match the natural, we took a few fish before the morning sun rose enough to drive the naturals off the water and into the grass.

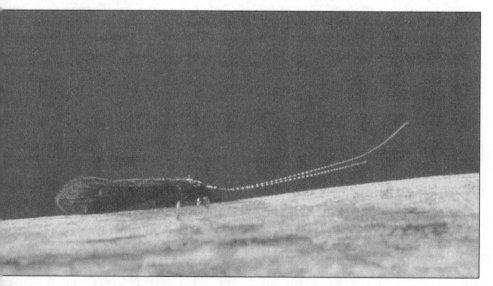

FIGURE 42 – MYSTACIDES ALAFIMBRIATA

This behavior is typical of *Mystacides* caddisflies. They will almost always be seen riding the surface in a resting position, calmly floating long distances. Trout rise to these floating naturals, and an adult pattern is always best.

Look for this caddis on some western spring creeks and the Henry's Fork from late July to early September.

Good fly patterns for the *Mystacides* are #16 gray X Caddis and Hemingway Caddis.

THE STONEFLIES: THEIR EMERGENCES AND ACTIVITY PERIODS

Stonefly activity brings anglers back to the West year after year. From the large salmonflies and golden stones to the tiny little yellow stoneflies, anglers often come from all over the world to meet and fish these emergences and egg-laying activities.

Salmonflies—Pteronarcys californica

This is the West's largest stonefly: Mature nymphs and adults may be 3 inches long. Nymphs live two to four years before emerging

FIGURE 43 – SALMONFLY ADULT

FIGURE 44 – SALMONFLY NYMPH

on our big western rivers. Just prior to hatching, the bellies of these chocolate-brownish-black nymphs turn a distinct orange, indicating that it is but a few days to emergence. Adults are orange with amber wings heavily veined in black.

Trout feed on the nymphal and adult stages of the salmonfly. Just before emerging, the nymphs migrate toward shore. The trout often follow this migration and feed on the nymphs near the banks for several days before the hatch. This activity is always reliable and offers good nymph fishing.

The hatch moves upriver several miles per day. When the females return to the water during egg-laying flights a few days later (like the emergence, this activity moves upstream each day), prime dry-fly fishing can be expected. You will do best if you find the spot where females are swarming.

Look for the salmonfly hatch to occur on heavy flows and rapids. Box Canyon on the Henry's Fork produces fine emergences and egg-laying flights during late May and early June. On the Madison River the hatch shows up during late June and moves upstream into early July. Firehole Canyon activity occurs in early June. The Gallatin's hatch gets going around the first week of July, as does the Yellowstone's.

Good fly patterns for salmonflies are #2–8 Brooks's, Nick's, and Black and Mature Nature Nymphs (put an orange belly on your fly to simulate the natural just prior to emergence), as well as #4–8 Henry's Fork Salmonflies and Jughead Adults.

Golden Stoneflies—Hesperoperla pacifica

Golden stones offer the best stonefly-fishing opportunities because they are available as adults longer than other species. The major species is the *Hesperoperla pacifica*. It's common to see them fluttering about on stretches of the Yellowstone River for a full two months. This and the fact that they hatch later in the season, when water conditions are more favorable, means that trout will rise to these insects more strongly than to salmonflies.

When no other surface feeding is apparent, fishing a golden stone adult pattern will raise a few trout on most streams' riffle water.

FIGURE 45 – GOLDEN STONEFLY ADULT

Nymphing anglers can consistently do well using nymphal imitations of this species, since they are always present. Nymphs require two to four years to mature.

Nymphs are #2 through #6; their coloration is mottled brown, yellow, and golden amber. Adults range a bit smaller—#4 through #8 —and are dirty gold in color.

Look for emergences on the Gardner, Henry's Fork, and Gallatin during late June and into July. On the Park's Yellowstone, the hatch occurs from mid-July through August.

Good fly patterns for golden stoneflies are #2–6 Brooks's, Nick's, and Golden Nature Stone Nymphs, as well as #4–8 Kaufmann's Stimulators and Henry's Fork Golden Stone Adults.

Little Yellow Stoneflies—Isoperla *species and* Suwallia pallidula

Little yellow stoneflies appear on many western rivers each summer. While you will not see a steady rise of fish to these #10 through #16 stoneflies, many trout can be taken on imitations.

Two species are common. The *Isoperla* species is the larger and has a dirty yellow abdomen that often features a red butt. The other,

FIGURE 46 – LITTLE YELLOW STONEFLY

Suwallia pallidula, is a beautiful #16 insect with an almost fluorescent yellow to lime body.

Emergences can occur on the Firehole and Madison Rivers in Yellowstone Park during June. On the Madison they can be fished from July through mid-August. On the Henry's Fork from below the Riverside campground to Ashton, Idaho, look for little yellow stoneflies to show during May and to last into July. Gallatin River little yellows start in July and emerge through August on selected stretches, as well as on several of its tributaries. Little yellow stones are a prolific insect and are present on most western streams with suitable habitat. The nymphs prefer riffles, pocket water, and canyon water, and emergences will be best in these places.

Good fly patterns for little yellow stoneflies are #10–16 Hare's Ears and Little Yellow Stonefly Nymphs. For your adult pattern use a #10–16 Little Yellow Stonefly.

DAMSELFLY
EMERGENCES AND ACTIVITY PERIODS

Damselflies thrive in most stillwaters of the West. Lakes, ponds, and sloughs always seem to have good populations, and damselflies are one of the most important insects for both fish and fishermen on these waters.

Several species of damsels inhabit waters I fish, yet they can be treated as one because their behavior is similar.

Nymphs are always long and slender, #6 through #10. Colors range from green and olive to brown and tan. Most are camouflaged to blend in with their surroundings. Most nymphs crawl out of the water to emerge on shore or on logs, float tubes, or anchor lines. Migrations of nymphs moving slowly toward shore are vulnerable to cruising trout.

Adult damselflies may be important to trout when the wind comes up or during mating. Trout take adults whenever they encounter them on the surface or find them flying near grassy banks. It's not uncommon to see trout leaping out of the water in hot pursuit of adult damsels flying along the shoreline.

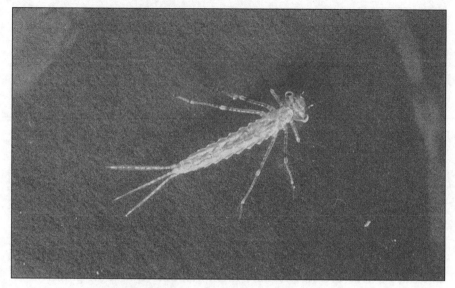

FIGURE 47 – DAMSELFLY NYMPH

July is the month for most damselfly activity in this area. Look for fine damsel activity anytime during the summer season on Henry's, Cliff, Wade, Grizzly, and Joffe Lakes. On streams such as the Firehole, ponds such as Blacktail Deer, and many of the unnamed sloughs and beaver-dammed waters, damsels are important from June through September.

Good fly patterns for damselflies are #6–10 B.S. and Henry's Lake Damsel Nymphs, as well as #10–12 Grebe and Henry's Lake Damselfly Adults.

MIDGES—
TINY AND OVERLOOKED INSECTS
WITH MIGHTY BIG EMERGENCES
FOR TROUT AND ANGLERS

The truth is that most anglers are like I used to be. They see midges on the water, and they may even know that they're being taken by rising trout. But they don't want to admit that there are times when trout will refuse almost every other insect in favor of midges.

Wherever trout are found, so are midges. They can be an important food source for trout on all waters. Anglers may overlook them in favor of larger insects, or they may refuse to believe that trout would rise to any insect so tiny, but trout like midges—big time. Get over avoiding fishing their minute imitations. Learn their habits, and with proper presentation strategies you, too, will be taking big rising trout on small midge patterns.

Members of the Chironomidae species can range in size from the huge #12 midges on Hebgen Lake to the tiny #26 green midges successfully fished on the Yellowstone River.

Midges are most important during their emergence, when fish rise to pupae and crippled adults. On some waters mating clusters can also be important.

Because they emerge year-round, you must be prepared to fish midges at all times. The actual presence of midges on the water is the best clue that trout are rising to them.

Lakes, ponds, and sloughs are rich with midges, which are near the top of the list of insects that rising trout might be feeding on. On streams the importance of midges usually varies with the season. The summer months bring on caddis, mayflies, and stoneflies, moving midges to near the bottom of the list of favored trout insects.

FIGURE 48 – MIDGE ADULT

From late fall into the spring season, however, midges may be the only aquatic insect emerging.

Midges are two-winged flies that come in a variety of sizes and colors. They can emerge on all waters any time of the day and season.

Be prepared with imitations of pupae and crippled adults and you will catch trout on midges.

Good fly patterns for midges are #10–26 Fur Midge Pupae, Serendipities, Zelon Midge Emergers, Cooper Bugs, Zelon Midges, Midge Clumps, and Griffith's Gnats.

TERRESTRIALS THAT BRING RISING TROUT ON ALL WATERS DURING THEIR TIME IN THE SUN

Landborne insects have no "emergences" or corresponding rises of trout. Rarely will a fly fisher encounter activity of any terrestrial insect concentrated enough to cause a rise of trout. Of course, there are exceptions: flying ants, mating bee swarms, and migrations of Mormon crickets.

Still, you must always be prepared to fish terrestrial imitations. I've taken trout on beetle patterns every month of the year because they're recognized as a food source and can be found near and sometimes on the water any time of the season.

Grasshopper activity is strongest during the heat of the summer months, but I've taken trout from May through November on

GOOD FLY PATTERNS FOR TERRESTRIALS:

Ants: #14–22 red and black Foam Ants, Zelon Flying Ants, and Parachute Ants.

Beetles: #10–18 Blue Ribbon Foam Beetles, Crystal Beetles, and Tiger and Box Elder Beetles.

Grasshoppers: #4–14 Dave's Hoppers, Schroeder's Parachute Hoppers, Pheasant Hoppers, and Chaos Hoppers.

Crickets: #4–12 Slough Creek Crickets and Dave's Crickets.

hopper patterns. Though hoppers are most prevalent in August and September, the fact is that they're often present on western waters for much longer. Grasshoppers are like tiny armored cars, burrowing in for several days to withstand snow and cold and appearing on stream again once the weather warms. Only a blanket of snow and cold of several days' duration will kill them.

Swarming bees and flying ants can bring tremendous rises of trout in Yellowstone country, especially in late July and August— though approaching a rise might be a bit unnerving with all the naturals buzzing about!

Flying ant swarms always bring rising trout on the Madison and Gallatin Rivers, several spring creeks, and some area lakes during mid-August.

The migrating Mormon cricket causes quite a stir on many waters during years when populations are strong. The females measure 2 to 3 inches long, and as they migrate across meadow areas many find their way into the water. I've heard reports of migrations during which a lead cricket jumped into the water and the others followed like lemmings. August and September are the best months for the cricket, although I've had fine action during June and October, too.

Be prepared for terrestrials whenever and wherever you are fishing western waters. This type of dry-fly angling can bring up the largest wild trout, and those who are ready for it can expect to do well.

OTHER FLY PATTERNS
FOR ANGLERS

Many locals still use Royal Wulffs and Trudes for searching waters when there are no rising trout. I know of several anglers who successfully fish a #16 Adams or Horner Deer Hair. Many only nymph-fish with general patterns that imitate no particular insect but may suggest several found in the waters. Following is a list of proven general flies for western waters:

OTHER FLY PATTERNS

General dry flies: #12–20 Adamses, #8–18 Horner Deer Hairs (Goofus Bugs), #8–18 Royal Wulffs and Royal Trudes, #10–18 H & L Variants.

General nymphs: #4–10 Crane Fly Larvae, #6–16 Prince Nymphs, #10–14 Zug Bugs, #10–16 Feather Dusters and Hare's Ear Nymphs, #4–12 leeches, #12–16 scuds, and #6–8 egg patterns, along with #12–16 Partridge and Peacock, Partridge and Primrose, and Pheasant Tail Soft Hackles.

Streamers: #2–10 Fly Fur Streamers, Soft-Hackle Streamers, Woolhead Sculpins, Muddler Minnows, Woolly Buggers, and Light Spruce Streamers.

PART FOUR

Yellowstone Country's Second Season

CHAPTER 7

Fall: The Prespawn—
A Special Time for Anglers

F all is the favorite time for most local anglers. Gone are the lines at gas pumps, grocery stores, and the two stop-lights in our town. Locals can again claim "their" seats at the restaurants and "their" parking spots along favorite trout waters. Bugling bull elk begin to gather their harems in the early-morning light. The hoarfrost is heavy on golden grass along the river where anglers are working riffles and pools. Thick clouds of mist float up and down the stream's silver course, blotting anglers from and into view as they move along.

I know that the first big male browns are moving up into the Madison River from Hebgen Lake when the trico mayfly emergence wanes where these two waters meet. Usually it's the last week in August, give or take a week—much earlier than most think. That's okay, because these fish won't feed when they first take to the cur-rents after easing around stillwaters for several months.

Fall brings some brown trout upriver from lakes in preparation for spawning. Other browns may drop downstream from lakes into stream outlets to spawn. Rainbow trout often follow the browns on their spawning migrations. Not to be denied are fall-spawning brook trout. Many times I've been startled by big brookies bolting after I spooked them as they quietly spawned in the slow flow below a beaver dam where I'd hoped to catch a few mallard ducks off guard.

Fall fishing to prespawning trout requires special strategies. Visiting anglers must first realize how fickle this type of angling can be and how difficult planning to meet it is.

Take, for instance, the fall 1995 season, which didn't produce good angling until the end of October. Fly fishers from all over the world began arriving on September 1 for fall action—but it was not forthcoming until almost two months later.

First, let's define *fall fishing* as "angling designed to take migrating fish *prior* to their spawning activities." To fish to trout that are actively spawning on redds is unsportsmanlike and should never be attempted. Trout must be allowed to spawn unmolested. Studies show that simply wading through a spawning bed can destroy most or all of the eggs.

Most years, the brown trout fall run begins with a few males starting upstream in mid-August. Do not plan on catching these fish. The first fish simply do not take flies readily. Instead, they move into deep protected pools and wait until the time is right. Rainbows often follow the browns up and behave the same way— not feeding, but just holding for several days.

There has been much speculation as to what causes migrating fish to feed or to become territorial and chase streamers, but no one really knows for sure. Talk with any angler and you'll hear such responses as: "It's the weather," or "It's ten nights where temperatures go below freezing," or "It's a full moon followed by a cold rain during the month of September." From my own observations I'd add that the later in September, the better, and late October is best.

Stream-by-stream variation is always a consideration when you're planning this type of fishing. For instance, on the Yellowstone River below Gardiner fall fishing for browns can begin in mid-September. On the Lewis River in Yellowstone Park, however, fall fishing can't be expected until after the first week in October. On the Madison above Hebgen Lake it may get going in early September, but it will be best a month later. The Madison below the lake never fishes well until late September. On the South Fork of the Madison I've never had fall fishing until mid-October. And again, while fall angling usually gets going around mid-September, in 1995 it didn't get off the ground until late October.

It's usually better to arrive here later in the season if you want to hit the run, but you must also keep in mind the closing dates of some waters, which can change yearly. One angler came in mid-November for fall action on Henry's Lake and the Madison in the Park only to discover that he was a couple of weeks too late to do so legally.

NOTES ON FALL STREAM FISHING

At certain times fall-run fish can be taken on all fly types. Much has been written on effective presentation using big nymphs and streamers. These methods are indeed effective, but there are others that can produce better during the right times.

Be alert to any insect emergence that brings up rises of fall fish. I was reminded of this a few years ago when Ronnie Hall and I arrived at the Mallard Rest camp on the Yellowstone River, upstream of Livingston.

I was telling Ronnie that on my first trip to this area, many years before, I'd watched Joe Brooks present an unweighted marabou streamer on a floating line to a run in the middle of the river. It was snowing at the time, and I can still see Joe throwing a long cast and then skittering the streamer along the surface using long, hard mends. He caught trout, and I was convinced for years afterward that this was the only presentation needed.

Ronnie and I geared up and hit the water. It was snowing, as it had so many years before, and I could almost see Brooks casting. But this day was different. There was no wind. It was so quiet you could almost hear the huge flakes fall through the grayness. We put our unweighted streamers on and headed into the swift Yellowstone. We had each taken a couple of small browns using Joe's technique when I decided to build a warm-up fire near one of the picnic tables next to the river. Wading ashore, I sloshed through a heavy hatch of fall *Baetis* that the fish were rising to. The mayflies were emerging and floating in the quieter currents behind the spot where we were wading and fishing streamers. So we changed tactics and took a few big browns in their spawning colors—more fish and larger fish than we'd been taking on streamers.

When fall fish become territorial before spawning, you can do better using floating lines and unweighted flies. Sinking lines catch on everything, and their bulk seems to be buoyed by the current, causing your flies to come to the surface anyway. So I stick with floating lines, and if I need weight I go with a weighted fly and/or put weight on my leader.

When fall-run browns and rainbows are territorial, you can present an unweighted streamer on a tight line across and down or up and across, then retrieve it with rapid, long strips. It's exciting to watch a trout come several feet to the surface to take your streamer with this method.

This type of presentation works best later in the season, when the trout are looking for anything to hit. Overcast conditions with precipitation are ideal, because trout become secure under cloud cover. That security, coupled with aggressive territorial behavior, brings on vicious takes.

During early-fall fishing or on bright days when the trout are reluctant to move far, you may want to try a weighted sculpin pattern using the same approach described above. Here, though, allow your fly to sink by mending once or twice. Try a slow retrieve or none at all. When the take comes, do not set the hook; allow the fish to hook himself. Usually a trout taking a sculpin imitation will hit the fly the first time to shock, stun, or immobilize it, then return to it immediately. If you strike, you may pull the fly away and eliminate his chances of taking it.

Another effective technique for taking fall-run fish is to present a big attractor dry fly such as a Royal Wulff or H & L Variant in likely holds. Fall fish can often be taken on terrestrial patterns, too.

I should mention here that fall fish, especially those up from lakes, require deeper water for security. Look for deep water near undercuts and overhangs, along with deep runs and bottom structure such as big rocks and boulders.

Presenting large nymphs and patterns that imitate whitefish and trout eggs can also be effective. Searching the water as you cast upstream and dead-drift these flies is a method that can be counted on. Stonefly nymphs or big attractors such as Princes, cranefly larvae, and others will be readily taken by fall fish.

SPEY RODS FOR FALL FISHING

A fairly new form of presenting to and covering western waters during fall fishing is that of using spey rod techniques. The spey rod allows presentations in areas where trees or other obstructions make backcasts impossible. Spey techniques give a fixed-length presentation without false casting, allowing each cast to fall into the same holding and security area. Your flies are before the trout rapidly and in precisely the right spot, making it much easier for them to accept your presentation. Spey techniques for western waters are just now evolving, with much experimentation currently taking place. They indeed will be a part of successful future western angling strategies.

Weather and Wind, and Their Effects on Western Fishing

Most professional entomologists tell us that mayflies should prefer to emerge during dry, warm conditions. But every experienced western angler knows that the best fly-fishing opportunities that mayfly emergences provide are on overcast and cool days. Misty, rainy, or snowy conditions are usually the ideal.

During inclement weather the insects ride the currents longer and thus suffer more crippling defects during hatching. As a result trout are given a longer and easier time to feed on these emergers and crippled duns. During heavy emergences fish become confident, locked into a feeding pattern and rhythm. They rise intensely, allowing you to approach closely. Precipitation also obscures trout vision, allowing a closer approach. Plus they just seem to *feel* more comfortable under overcast skies.

Mayfly spinners do require warm, calm mornings or evenings to mate and lay their eggs, however. Any precipitation or heavy wind may prevent them from reaching the water.

Warm, calm mornings and evenings seem to produce the most active periods for caddisflies, whether the insects are emerging or laying eggs. There are times when wind causes problems for egg-laying females as they skitter along on the surface; it can knock them back into the water when they have deposited an egg mass and are trying to get airborne again. Here the trout may recognize the caddisflies' dilemma and key in on struggling caddis trapped in the surface film.

Stoneflies emerge in sunny conditions, although prime dry-fly fishing to stonefly activity usually occurs during egg-laying periods. For this activity always look to sunny, warm, and windy days.

Damselflies prefer the same weather conditions as stoneflies for emerging. Damselfly mating activity can be best on sunny, warm days when the wind is howling. This forces adults off the shorelines and, often, into the water, where trout gather in anticipation.

Midge emergences on lakes and stillwaters are always heaviest during calm, warm periods. I like overcast conditions best, but it makes no difference to the insects whether it's overcast or bright. Still, from the angler's standpoint, fishing midges is best when it's overcast, because you can approach rising trout more closely, and there's less shadow from lines and glint from rods. Midges, too, are subject to emergence defects, with cripples common in the heaviest hatches. Here, inclement weather usually causes even more problems for emerging midges and allows trout a better opportunity to feed on cripples.

During mating periods when midges cluster in clumps, blustery weather conditions may force these mating clumps to the shore, where fish will concentrate to take them.

Ants, bees, beetles, crickets, and grasshoppers seem to prefer sunny, warm weather to conduct their business of swarming, mating, and egg laying. Generally, these insects seem most active on nice days. Windy, warm, sunny days often carry terrestrials onto the water's surface. Sometimes terrestrials become concentrated near the water when they find suitable habitat. They also concentrate during mating swarms and migrations that bring them near the water. Windy, warm, sunny weather can yield fine terrestrial activity and fishing. And even though it freezes during a few nights in late

August and September, most terrestrials will remain available to trout until snow and cold permanently seal their fate under a layer of white.

During the late season, when anglers think of fall-run trout, it's always best to try streamer or nymph fishing when the clouds are low and it's either raining or snowing. If it's going to be a sunny day, get to the river early—well before the sun's rays hit the water and drive the fish into the security of the deepest pools. Sunny days mean spooky fish. Trout up from lakes such as Hebgen are used to the security afforded by deeper lake water. When these trout enter rivers and streams, the noises and shadows they encounter can cause skittishness and extreme caution. An overcast sky or precipitation keeps shadow problems down, and trout seem to feel more comfortable and are easier to approach. If it has been a sunny day, wait until the sun begins to set before you search pools and runs with your flies. It always helps to have all the sun's rays off the water before you search it for fall fish. While a few trout can be taken on sunny days, it's better to try for them on those overcast, rainy-snowy days when most folks stay inside. As for me, I'll be out trying to bring on another chilblain—and in doing so experience some of the finest fishing the West can offer.

DEALING WITH AFTERNOON WINDS

The cow moose and her calf drink from their own shadows on the calm, reflective surface of the pond next to the Basin Ranger Station. It's mid-July. High pressure rules the Rockies, bringing clear blue skies on calm, crisp mornings. These conditions usually last until September's equinox storms replace the almost-permanent high pressure that's been with us all summer. These placid mornings provide anglers with fine gulper fishing on area lakes. Trout freely rise to mayflies on a surface so smooth that it mirrors the big blue Montana sky.

Around noon, though, a light wind might begin. Now and then the first easy winds of the day come and go for an hour or two.

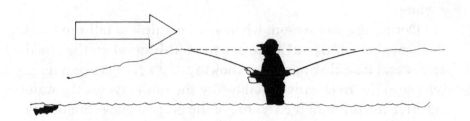

FIGURE 49 – SHORT-LINE WIND CASTING

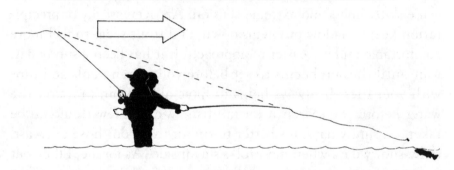

FIGURE 50 – BACKHAND WIND CASTING

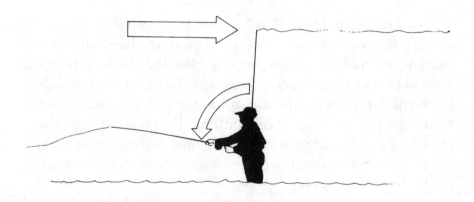

FIGURE 51 – POWER-FORWARD STROKE

These spurts of wind are the result of air masses beginning to change altitude and temperature. As the sun climbs and temperatures rise further, convectional winds begin to crank up in earnest. If you happen to be in a float tube when the convectional winds blow in, it might be too late to paddle home if you have to go against them. You could be blown to the opposite side of the lake, forcing a long walk back to your car. Once the initial winds come up, start fishing your way back toward the parking area and stay close to it in your tube thereafter so that once the convection winds arrive for the day you can get off the water.

The howling afternoon gales also cause many technical difficulties with effective approach and presentation. Making an accurate cast in these conditions might seem a chimerical goal, but it can be done.

The vicious afternoon winds we often experience on western waters make it nearly impossible to present casts from your casting-hand side. These winds must be dealt with much differently than standard winds. First, get as close to your target as possible. A short-line cast is your first defense in overcoming western winds. Next, keep your casting plane low. The wind is always more intense above your head, so keep your casts at head level, or lower if possible. Now, try to position yourself so that your presentation will be to the downwind side, not straight into the teeth of the gusts. Try a backhand cast by casting backward: Your backcast thus becomes your presentation.

If you can't get into position to deliver a backhand cast and find yourself having to cast into the wind, do this: If it's a downstream gale and you're able to approach from below, get as close to your target as possible. Work out a short fixed length of line—about 15 feet from rod tip to fly. Allow the wind to fully extend your line, leader, and tippet behind you so that it all merely sails in the wind. Now, with a power-forward stroke, bring the cast into the wind and to your target. The rod is preloaded, so to speak, by the wind, not by your backcast. This line-extension cast is a fine tool for vicious wind situations.

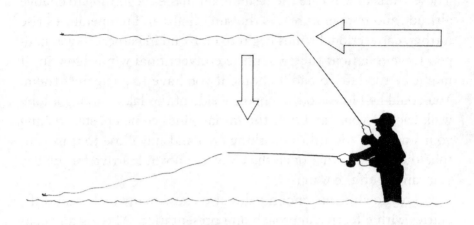

FIGURE 52 – NONCAST

If your presentation must be made into an upstream wind, sim-ply approach from downstream and allow your extension of line, leader, tippet, and fly to float on the gale so that it hovers just upstream of your intended target. Now, drop this noncast to the water, ideally allowing just the tippet to fall near the target so as not to line the trout or holding water you are searching.

Be flexible. When one method fails to defeat afternoon winds, try another. Or, with some practice, an ambidextrous approach is best.

You don't need monster rods and heavy weight-forward lines to defeat nasty winds. Shorter rods—7- to 8-1/2-footers—keep backcasts lower, causing less wind resistance. Lighter lines also mean less wind resistance because of their smaller diameter and the lighter weight of the rod itself. And since double-taper and weight-forward lines are usually the same diameter for the first 30 feet, it makes no difference which one you cast. Neither performs better than the other at these presentation distances.

When it comes to leader-tippet length, I shorten my normally longer, finer leaders during heavy winds. While searching the water or fishing insect activity with #12 and smaller flies, a 9-foot leader with 2 or 3 feet of 4X or 5X tippet is a fine rig. Pitching larger flies such as salmonfly dries or big cricket or grasshopper patterns requires 9-foot leaders tapered to 4X or 5X to turn over into these winds. When nymphing or throwing larger streamers, I often go with a 6-foot leader tapered to a 1X or 0X tippet.

CHAPTER 9

The Future:
Final Thoughts and Notes

T he future of western fly fishing is brighter today than it was yesterday. While occasionally we have too many anglers trying to fish the same water at the same time, producing conflict, western angling has never been better.

A number of things contribute greatly to the continued health of our rivers: Progressive fisheries programs, progressive management of our public lands, better-educated anglers and politicians, stronger strains of wild trout, and pollution controls and greenbelt restrictions prohibiting building on the riverbanks are some examples.

Organizations such as The Nature Conservancy of Idaho, Montana, and Wyoming, the Montana Land Reliance, and others help secure conservation easements along the rivers. These easements forever protect wild trout habitat and keep the land intact and free from subdivisions—which might bring more homes and potential for harmful development to our river corridors.

Progressive regional leaders of agencies such as the United States Forest Service are thinking more about recreational opportunities, such as fishing, than about forestry when managing our public lands. In their "Forest Plans" we now see "fishing and wild trout habitat potential and protection" mentioned more often than "millions of board feet of timber." These leaders are closing roads and environmentally sensitive areas to protect them from abuse—and are thus coming under attack from special-interest groups that want these lands open to every use, no matter what the cost to the environment and its wild inhabitants. Let's support the people and organizations who are protecting our trout habitat. Send them a letter or drop by and visit, letting them know how they are doing. Without their often-courageous stances, our sport could suffer irreparable damage.

Groups such as the Greater Yellowstone Coalition, Henry's Fork Foundation, Madison-Gallatin Wild Trout Foundation, and Montana Trout Foundation are protecting and preserving wild trout habitat through their persistent and valiant efforts. Again, without these groups our sport would suffer greatly. Please join and support them.

The more we allow the elimination of wet and wild places, the less we are able, in good faith, to pick up rod and reel and take to the waters that are left.

A Selected
Bibliography

T he books listed here are only some of those I've used to help develop effective fly-fishing strategies. A few have only small amounts of information on fishing strategies but are wonderful reads in themselves.

Back, Howard. *The Waters of Yellowstone with Rod and Fly*. New York: Dodd, Mead, and Co., 1938.

Bergman, Ray. *Trout*. New York: The Penn Publishing Co., 1938.

Brooks, Charles E. *Fishing Yellowstone Waters*. New York: Lyons & Burford,* 1984.

_____. *Larger Trout for the Western Fly Fisherman*. Cranbury, N.J.: A. S. Barnes and Co., 1970.

_____. *The Living River*. New York: Lyons & Burford,* 1979.

_____. *Nymph Fishing for Larger Trout*. New York: Crown Publishers, 1976.

_____. *The Trout and the Stream*. New York: Lyons & Burford,* 1974.

Brooks, Joe. *Trout Fishing*. New York: Times Mirror Magazines, Inc., 1972.

Haines, Aubrey L. *The Yellowstone Story*. 2 vols. Mammoth, Wyo.: The Yellowstone Library and Museum Association with Colorado Associated University Press, 1976-77.

Harding, Col. E. W. *The Fly Fisher and the Trout's Point of View*. Philadelphia: J. B. Lippincott Co., 1931.

Juracek, John and Craig Mathews. *Fishing Yellowstone Hatches*. West Yellowstone, Mont.: Blue Ribbon Flies, 1992.

LaFontaine, Gary. *Caddisflies*. New York: Lyons & Burford,* 1981.

Lyons, Nick. *Bright Rivers*. New York: J. B. Lippincott Co., 1977.

_____. *Confessions of a Fly Fishing Addict*. New York: Simon & Schuster, 1989.

_____. *Spring Creek*. New York: Atlantic Monthly Press, 1992.

Mathews, Craig and Clayton Molinero. *The Yellowstone Fly-Fishing Guide*. New York: Lyons & Burford,* 1997.

Mathews, Craig and John Juracek. *Fly Patterns of Yellowstone*. West Yellowstone, Mont.: Blue Ribbon Flies, 1987.

Pierce, Steve. *The Lakes of Yellowstone*. Seattle: The Mountaineers, 1987.

Roemhild, George. *Aquatic Insects of Yellowstone*. Mammoth, Wyo.: The Yellowstone Institute, 1983.

Schwiebert, Ernest. *Nymphs*. New York: Winchester Press, 1973.

Staples, Bruce. *River Journal—Yellowstone Park*. Portland, Ore.: Frank Amato Publishers, 1996.

Swisher, Doug and Carl Richards. *Fly Fishing Strategy*. New York: Crown Publishers, 1975.

Varley, John and Paul Schullery. *Freshwater Wilderness*. Mammoth, Wyo.: The Yellowstone Library and Museum Association, 1983.

Walker, Richard. *Trout Fishing*. North Pomfret, Vt.: David & Charles Publishers, 1982.

* Lyons & Burford, Publishers changed its name to The Lyons Press in 1997.

Index